F

Also by Linda Georgian

Create Your Own Future

Communicating with the Dead

Your Guardian Angels

If You Really Want to Do It Right: Try It the Wholistic Way

How to Attract Your Ideal Mate

Linda Georgian

A Fireside Book

Published by Simon & Schuster

F

FIRESIDE
Rockefeller Center
1230 Avenue of the Americas
New York, NY 10020

FIRESIDE and colophon are registered trademarks
of Simon & Schuster, Inc.

Designed by Jennifer Daddio

Manufactured in the United States of America

1   3   5   7   9   10   8   6   4   2

Library of Congress Cataloging-in-Publication Data
Georgian, Linda M.
How to attract your ideal mate/Linda Georgian.
p.   cm.
"A Fireside Book"
1. Mate selection.   2. Man–woman relationships.   3. Love.   4. Interpersonal attraction.
5. Interpersonal relations—Psychic aspects.   I. Title.
HQ801.G395 1999   98-42246
646.7'7—dc21   CIP
ISBN 0-684-85021-4

Acknowledgments

Anytime you're writing a book, it comes to fruition because of the love, support, and encouragement of so many others. I want to thank Jim Anderson, for always being there to pray with me and help me realize God's plan is in divine order; my attorney, Eric Cheshire, for helping me through the legal maze; Irving and Marge Cowan, for being lifelong friends and supporting me and my mission to help others; Nina L. Diamond, an editor who always has the creative insight to make sure everything is done right; my literary agent, Lynn Franklin, who's also a spiritual friend and has the insight and expertise to guide my literary career; Peter Green, my manager and legal eagle, who helps me get the peace of mind to accomplish my mission; Jocelyn Greenky, from *George* magazine, who's a wonderful, supportive friend and my New York soul sister; Brian Hartline, whose support has helped me realize many of my dreams, including attracting my ideal mate; my personal assistant, Diane, and her husband, Chris Hurst, for always being by my side through the ups and downs without fail.

Thank you to writer Pam Johnson, for her upbeat personality and for being attuned to my thoughts and helping me put them on paper; my Simon & Schuster editor, Sydny Miner, for being an inspiration by creating an ideal relationship and making writing this book such a wonderful experience; my loving friend John Nero, for the years he has been my human angel; Sandra and Patti Post, my sister and niece, for their constant support and belief in my abilities; my hypnotherapist, Frank Rocco, for always being there and for helping me attract my ideal mate; Jim Ryan, for being my ideal mate; my favorite nephew, Daniel Silagy, for all of his Web site help, and his wife, Deborah, for using these techniques to create their perfect relationship and inspiring others; Curtis Skoda, who's a kindred brother, my maintenance angel, and has been by my side helping me with absolutely everything for many years.

My gratitude goes to Masanori Sugiura, my Japanese connection and close friend, who's been a constant help in, and helps me achieve, my mission in Japan; Mr. Yamasaki and his staff, for being like a loving family when I'm in Japan and for all of their assistance with the personal and business arrangements.

My deepest thanks to my late mother, Marie Georgian Simmons, who still guides me, gave me my psychic gift, and has been the inspiration for my life, and to my late father, Anthony Georgian, who always loved and supported me. I know they're sharing their ideal relationship on the other side. Special thanks to my dogs, Pekingese Smarty and Star, for keeping my spirits up and entertaining me. And finally to God, Jesus, the angels, and the saints, for having given me the gift of being able to help other people.

Contents

Part Two

Part Three

Introduction

Falling in love is actually a powerful experience of feeling the Universe move through you. The other person has become a channel for you, a catalyst that triggers you to open up to the love, beauty and compassion within.

SHAKTI GAWAIN

From the moment I opened up to my friends in college about my psychic gift, the questions I've been asked the most have been about love and relationships. Everyone wants to know: "When will I meet my soulmate?" "Am I dating him now?" "Will I ever hear from him/her again?" Or, "Where can I find my ideal mate?" Each person is looking to find their ideal mate to share in their journey. Without love, people feel empty and lonely.

Love is the nutrition required by our souls to energize us toward achieving our purpose on Earth. That's why it feels so good. When we're in love, we feel as if there's nothing we can't accomplish. Our bodies, minds, and souls are healthier. It's no wonder that if you're not in love, you *want* to be. And that's why we're driven to take the risks necessary to find our ideal mate: we go on blind dates, answer personal ads, read books, attend classes, call psychics, and pray to find our soulmate.

The process of finding your ideal mate is an opportunity to learn about yourself and your purpose in life.

Finding your ideal mate is more than just universal coincidence. It's true that most people meet their ideal mates unexpectedly, but that meeting is a by-product of the energy that you've been reflecting to the

Universe for a long, long time. The journey toward finding your ideal mate begins with knowing, respecting, and loving yourself first. My beloved mother, Marie Georgian Simmons, told me when I was growing up that it was important to develop myself as a person. This would then allow me to attract another complete person into my life. She said, "The most important earthly relationship that you have is with *yourself.*"

It's important to understand what you *really* want in a relationship at any given point in your life, because that's what you are going to attract. A friend of mine was recently divorced, and she often said that she was looking for someone to have fun with but not have a committed, ongoing relationship with. The men who kept appearing in her life were also interested in a noncommitted relationship. Eventually she complained that none of the men she was dating wanted more than a casual relationship. I reminded her that she was fond of saying that she wanted only fun, without commitment. That's the message she was presenting to the Universe, and that's what she was getting. At some point she changed her mind about what she wanted, but she didn't change her request to the Universe. As we move through different phases of our life, the definition of an ideal mate will also change to meet our changing needs.

During certain times of your life you may enjoy the lessons you can learn from dating many different people. You may also believe that there's one ideal mate for you, and you will put your time and energy into creating and maintaining that relationship. Sometimes you may think you've sent out one request and you wonder why you keep receiving something else. This is when you must take an inventory of your *true* beliefs about relationships and your ideal mate.

The Universe is always listening to our requests. A couple of years ago a colleague of mine had been dating a man for about a year, but he had not yet expressed his feelings about their relationship, or whether he even wanted to explore the possibilities of it continuing in the future. Driving down the highway one afternoon, in exasperation, she said out loud, "All right, I'm tired of this. I want to know what he wants!" Much to her surprise—although she shouldn't have been shocked, since she had directly asked the Universe for information—

her boyfriend, over dinner that evening, and without any hint from her, not only brought up the subject but volunteered quite emotionally that he cared deeply for her and wanted the relationship to last.

While some people might term this a coincidence, many of us know that when we ask for information or make our feelings known to what we loosely refer to as the Universe, or God, or whatever we choose to call the creative force we are intertwined with, we will get an answer, and often quite quickly. Somebody or something "out there" is always listening—and is indeed *here* to assist you. As many spiritual leaders have stated, the Universe conspires to fulfill all our dreams.

As the following story shows, you can send verbal or nonverbal messages to the Universe that you wish had not been sent. These, too, demonstrate the enormous power we have to manifest anything.

When one of my clients began dating a man she found herself in love with a few years ago, he was afraid because of the strong feelings he had for her. It had been many years since he had given up on the idea that he might find his ideal mate, and in the meantime he had married someone who he knew wasn't ideal for him. After that marriage faltered and he met my client, he realized that she was everything he had been looking for and that they were the "perfect fit." My client felt that way, too.

So, what was the problem?

The man, after expressing his deep feelings, seemed to stall the relationship. Knowing that he was afraid, my client was very patient, understanding, and encouraging. One evening, upon the advice of a friend, she drew pictures of everything she wanted at that point in her life. In addition to a few drawings related to her career, she drew on the page a picture of the man and herself holding hands. Around them she drew a shining sun, a palm tree, a beach——a beautiful romantic setting. On her left hand she drew an engagement ring and wedding band. To make sure that their identities couldn't possibly be misunderstood, she even put their initials as monograms on the T-shirts she had drawn on their figures.

For a couple of days the picture sat on the counter in her kitchen, but feel-

ing a bit embarrassed and not wanting anyone else to see the picture (for fear they might think her superstitious, childish, or even crazy), she put the picture on the top shelf in her bedroom closet next to some sweaters.

She had not told the man about this picture. In fact, the only one who knew about it was the friend who suggested she draw it in the first place.

Within forty-eight hours of her placing the picture on the shelf, the man she had been dating told her that he was afraid of his feelings and needed more time to think about their situation.

"I'm going to have to put you on a shelf for a little while," he told her.

When she heard those words she froze, in shock that he had chosen the phrase *on the shelf.* When she got home that night she immediately took the picture off the shelf in the closet and brought it back out into the bedroom.

"I stood there with the picture in my hand," she told me. "I had no idea where to put it next. I could not believe how much power this picture actually turned out to have."

She moved the picture from place to place around her house for the next couple of weeks, making sure it never sat on anything that even remotely resembled a shelf. She then said a little prayer, affirming her love for this man, and asked the Universe to bring them together again. Finally, she threw the picture away, releasing the power of the picture to the Universe.

Within a few months, he had taken her "off the shelf," and their relationship resumed.

Another example happened to a client of mine fifteen years ago, while he sat in a restaurant with a friend having ice cream.

"I know what I'm looking for," he told his friend, "but I just haven't found her yet."

"Me, too," his friend replied.

"Why don't we try something just for fun?" my client suggested. "Each of us can write down every single quality and detail we can think of that describes the woman each of us is looking for, and then let's read out loud what's on our list."

They each grabbed a napkin and wrote down their list. They left no stone unturned. In fact, they both felt a bit silly because their lists included the time *of year they thought their ideal mate's birthday would be, what her hands would look like, and even the tiniest details about her family, interests, and life's work.*

They read their lists aloud to each other and my client said to his friend, "Well, if I run into your girl, I'll send her to you; and if you run into mine, send her to me."

The very next afternoon, my client met a woman through his work. They began dating a week later, and he soon discovered she matched everything on the ice cream napkin list.

They were married two and a half years later.

This book highlights all of the principles I've learned and taught people throughout my career as a psychic and spiritual advisor. I also show examples of real relationships people have had, either learning about the types of relationship they want to have (their own individual spiritual lessons) or actually meeting and beginning their journeys with their soulmates.

In Part One we focus on the Law of Love. You must first love yourself so you can give love to others. Relationships with ideal mates are based on many types of love, depending on what you need and want at that time in your life. We'll discuss why you must become a whole person and live in a state of love to create the energy to attract your ideal mate.

In Part Two we explore the Law of Preparation and Attraction. Preparing yourself by learning what you want and need in a relationship is necessary in order to attract what you *really* want in a mate and in a relationship. Often we put energy into creating one thing even though we really want something else. It's like ordering cheese pizza and, when it arrives, expecting there to be pepperoni on it. You must make certain that what you want and what you request are the same thing.

In Part Three we see that once you've found your ideal mate, it's important to practice the Law of Maintenance. You must nurture your relationship to provide mutual growth that enhances its spiritual, emotional, mental, and physical aspects. I'll help you identify ways to develop a relationship from the moment you meet a possible life mate until you're both ready to make that commitment. Even relationships with ideal mates require effort and care to ensure that the romance continues to bloom.

In Part Four we focus on the Law of Letting Go. Some relationships are part of our growing process as spiritual beings but aren't meant to last a lifetime. Just because a relationship didn't last forever, though, doesn't mean that the other person wasn't your ideal mate for that particular moment in time. This chapter will also reveal how to lovingly let go of past relationships so you can move forward and begin new ones.

In each chapter you'll meet clients to whom I've taught the principles of attracting their ideal mate and others who've shared their stories about their relationships with me. You'll see the principles of these universal laws in action through these real life stories about people who've loved, grown wiser, and have experienced being in a relationship with an ideal mate. Your heart and soul will be inspired as you begin to believe it can happen to you.

Remember, your will is very powerful. As you literally create your life, think about this:

In this world there are only two tragedies. One is not getting what one wants, and the other is getting it.

OSCAR WILDE

Part One

Law of Love

Love isn't something that we find, it's something that we do.
CLINT BLACK, SOMETHING THAT WE DO

*For one human being to love another: that is perhaps the most
difficult of all our tasks, the ultimate, the last test and proof,
the work for which all other work is but preparation.*
RAINER MARIA RILKE

What's the only four-letter word you can't hear enough of? *Love.* We all want to feel it, hear it, and experience it. We search the world looking for it. We hope and pray to find it. We go to psychics, seminars, dating services, church, and therapy; read books; and have countless dates trying to find it or the map that leads to it. We'd be only so thrilled if the Home Shopping Network could package it and sell it and UPS could deliver it to our door.

Everyone knows why we take risk after risk searching for it. There's no greater feeling in the world than being in love. Love is the most potent natural aphrodisiac. Food, alcohol, or drugs can't replace it. It's a healer. It's our connection to the universal forces of life, or God.

Love is the gatekeeper that allows us to experience all other emotions. Without love we surround our hearts with a stone wall and eventually can't feel anything, until the wall is torn down. Love is what allows us to feel joy and sorrow; it gives us laughter and tears, provides strength for others and the need to be held. Love is a state of being that allows us to experience all things. It's not something that you find; it's a way of life.

Someone looking for the love of their life must have a clear understanding of what love *is* in their life. Think of love as a house. Self-love is the foundation of your house. If you have a weak love foundation, the house will be shaky. On the other hand, if you have a solid, strong love foundation, you have the opportunity to build a house full of more love in your life than you can imagine. The fact that you have self-love doesn't mean that you won't have to say no to some of the people trying to put inferior-quality materials in your house of love. There are always con artists out there testing us to see if we'll put things in our house of love that aren't healthy or don't match our requirements. However, if you have a strong foundation you'll have less to rebuild or will be able to recover more quickly if you accidentally put inferior products in your house.

Fortunately, you can always improve or change your foundation. In fact, keeping your foundation strong is a lifelong job. Different parts of your foundation may be weak at different times in your life. Sometimes you may have to work more on the foundation that supports your family; other times, on taking care of yourself; and yet other times, on the foundation of your relationship with your significant other. It seems some rooms of a house are used more than others, and the foundation that supports them may need more maintenance. But by constantly maintaining your foundation you'll get to spend most of your moments living in the flow of love.

When you're living in a state of love, life is an adventure. Each day life offers experiences that are full of opportunities to enjoy living on Earth. Living in love is about living in the moment. With rare exceptions, when you're focusing on the moment you're living in, not on the past or future, you can be happy and in a state of love. Love is the most abundant natural resource we have.

When you're living in a state of love, it's difficult to be angry, resentful, and bitter. Unfortunately, we live in a culture that likes to take inventories of people's actions and keep debits and credits. Some good deeds get a credit, and every offense receives a debit. At some point in

our relationship we look at the balance sheet and see if we think everything has been fair. In a perfect world, debits and credits would always
be balanced. However, we live on planet Earth. Everyone here is participating in a human experience and has to learn their individual spiritual
lessons, so we create relationships in which the debits and the credits
aren't always equal.

Even when you feel your debits and credits aren't equal, you can still
access your infinite supply of love. It heals you so you can move forward. Of course, it's easier to access your infinite supply of love when
you're living in a state of self-love.

What Is Self-Love?

To fall in love with yourself is the first secret of happiness. I did so at the age
of four-and-a-half. Then if you're not a good mixer you can
always fall back on your own company.
ROBERT MORLEY

The best example of living in a state of self-love is a baby. Love is the essence of a baby's very being. You can feel it when you hold babies. They live in the moment. If they need food, a dry diaper, or someone to hold them, they let you know. When their need is met, you get a big grin, plenty of cooing, and a twinkle in their eyes. They explore without fear of the unknown. Each discovery—finding their toes, watching lights, chewing on their toys—is a source of great delight. They aren't thinking, "Yesterday I'd have been cuter if I'd worn a different bib," or, "I was thinner before," or, "I'm having a bad hair day." When they're learning to walk and they fall down, they get up and keep trying because learning something new is an adventure. Falling wasn't failure; it was just a moment in the past that is part of the process necessary to eventually learn how to run. Babies, of course, are not yet aware of society's pressures, judgments, and criticisms, which can so often challenge our ability to love and accept ourselves.

Self-love begins with looking in the mirror and liking whom and what you see. It's being kind and patient with yourself; after all, you, like everyone else, are a work in progress. Self-love is taking care of and developing yourself to be the best person you can be. It's about being a productive member of the human race. It's about living in the moment and liking who you are and what you're doing.

If you want to be a productive member of the human race, the first thing you have to do is take care of your physical self. Otherwise you burn out, and everyone else around you also suffers the consequences. When you are exhausted, unhealthy, and stressed, it's next to impossible to find peace, serenity, and anything resembling the feeling of love. We all know that taking care of our physical bodies means getting plenty of rest, eating right, and exercising. It means limiting or eliminating the intake of unhealthy substances like alcohol, drugs, nicotine, fast food, and sugar. Unfortunately, we often put our physical health at the bottom of our priority list, when it is a gift from God that should be cherished and nurtured. If you're exhausted, listen to your body crying out for a day of rest, and respond. If a baby were crying you wouldn't decide not to give it what it needed just because you were too busy. You'd comfort the baby. So, give yourself the same consideration. The fact that you've learned how to communicate without crying at the top of your lungs doesn't mean your soul isn't crying out with equal intensity for you to take care of yourself. Not taking care of yourself physically separates you from your ability to find self-love.

If you're not living in a state of self-love, it's very difficult to receive love. Think about when you spill something on your kitchen counter. You get a sponge to wipe it up. But first you wet the sponge. If you don't wet the sponge, it takes longer for the sponge to absorb the spilled liquid on the counter, because the sponge has a hard, crusty texture. You're a lot like a sponge. If you're filled with love, it's easier to receive it from others. If you're jaded, it takes longer for you to absorb love from others—not only your romantic partner but family, friends, and even life itself. If you aren't in love with living life, it's hard to find a partner in love with life.

When you're living a whole, balanced life it's easier to love life and living. It helps you grow and develop as a person. You'll meet new people, make new friends, and learn about yourself in the process.

Diane married her first husband when she was in her early twenties because she believed it was time to get married. She knew she wasn't supposed to marry a party boy, like the one she dated in college, so she married a responsible hard worker, who was also boring and didn't show any affection toward her or the children. "After ten years," she said, "I thought I was going to shrivel up and die because none of my emotional needs were getting met. The thought of growing old with him was more than I could handle, so I left. I had also started drinking too much."

Diane's second husband was the exact opposite: he was fun and affectionate, but could never keep a job. He was also an active alcoholic. There was tremendous pressure on Diane because she had to work harder and harder to keep them financially above water. She had a successful business, but it was killing her to work so hard during the day and party at night. Diane did this for eleven years before admitting she couldn't continue with this life, because she was too tired.

At that point Diane went into a recovery center for alcoholism and began her life in recovery. She decided she was going to make healthy choices about lifestyle and have healthier relationships. Once she went into recovery, she began to trust again, but she trusted the wrong people.

Her next relationship was with a man who was mature, polished, educated, and well-off. He worked in the recovery field, so she believed she could trust him to be honest. He kept her head spinning by buying her gifts and taking her to wonderful places. For a long time she didn't worry about where the relationship was going, but eventually she found out this relationship was based on lies. He had lied about being divorced and having a terminal illness, just to name a few things.

Diane became scared that she didn't know how to have a healthy relationship, and she was afraid she'd just leave this only to end up in another bad one.

That year she spent New Year's Eve alone. That night she decided she'd had enough of her boyfriend's lies and was going to end the relationship.

"It took me a few weeks to work through my feelings of anger and hatred toward him," Diane said. "I was also in the process of selling my business, so my life was very stressful."

One day at a support group meeting, Ed asked her to coffee. She'd met him three years earlier but really didn't know him very well. Within a week they began dating.

Within two months Ed and Diane were very serious. Diane realized she had someone who was there for her if she was sick or had car problems. She felt safe for the first time ever in a relationship. It was a new experience for her.

"I'd made it clear in the beginning I wasn't interested in a dead-end relationship," Diane said. "If this relationship was good, I wanted to know if he was interested in a permanent relationship. If he wasn't, then I didn't want to waste my time."

They dated for six months and then got married.

"The experience made me realize that sometimes when you're in the middle of a storm, you really can't see what's coming after it," Diane said. "Once I took myself out of a bad situation there was room for something positive to come into my life."

Even though Diane and Ed are both retired, many days go by that they go their separate ways. At the end of the day they share what happened.

Diane realizes the real pleasures come from small things: someone bringing you coffee or giving you a peck on the check "just because." That's what love is about for her.

People often comment, "Too bad you two didn't meet years earlier." But Diane and Ed realize that if they had met years ago, it would not have worked. Ed was traveling back then, and Diane would have hated raising children on her own. They were both previously active alcoholics.

While they were dating they gave each other a gift that was engraved, Timing is everything. "We both believe it was all part of God's plan," Diane explains.

Whole, Balanced Life: The Foundation for Self-Love

When we cling to another, we lose ourselves and become their person. When we let go, we find ourselves and become our own person. Only then is love possible.
SUSAN JEFFERS

I've always believed and taught that you must develop yourself as a person before you can attract your ideal mate. To help you do this, you need to be living a balanced life. You can't place all your growth emphasis in one area of your life. By this I mean you can't spend twenty-four hours a day just looking for love, or working, or taking care of your children. You have to develop other interests and talents. You even have to walk through some of the emotional issues you're scared of. I call it cleaning the cobwebs out of your emotional closet. Life is a mirror: you'll attract people who share your best and worst traits. By continually improving yourself you'll be strengthening your best traits, which will enable you to meet others who mirror those aspects.

When I read *Feel the Fear and Do It Anyway* by Dr. Susan Jeffers, it explained the concept of a balanced, whole life in a beautiful and simple way. She asks you to draw a box with nine smaller boxes inside. Each of the nine boxes represents an area of your life that you should spend time developing. Since we live in a practical world, you can't possibly spend an equal amount of time in each box every day. The fact is, you'll always be prioritizing the areas of your life that get more attention, based on your needs at the time. It's not about the amount of time you spend developing each box, but about being aware and prioritizing the need to develop yourself in all different areas of your life and actually doing it. If you're having fun in a particular area of life, you'll make more time for it.

Dr. Jeffers suggests that to create a whole life you need to develop your life in the following areas: contribution, hobby, leisure, family, alone time, personal growth, career, significant relationship, and friends.

- *Contribution.* This is what you give to others. It may mean volunteering for your child's Scout troop, being a Big Brother or Big Sister, or helping a neighbor. It doesn't have to mean saving the world. It should be something you do with the pure intent of its being a gift. Gifts are things given without any expectations of receiving anything, including emotional rewards.
- *Hobby.* This is something you do for pure enjoyment. It's not something that stresses you out; instead, it helps you release stress. That means you don't constantly criticize, critique, or compare how you're doing. Your hobby might be playing golf, painting, or taking a dance class. Whatever it is, make certain you have fun and laugh, and that time flies when you're doing it.
- *Leisure.* This is allowing yourself to relax when you're alone— not just relaxing when you're with friends, but just enjoying yourself. You might watch a movie or read a book for fun (this doesn't include self-help materials). You might want to sit on your front porch and look at the stars. Leisure means something relaxing: you're not looking for solutions to problems, trying to figure out the why of anything, or cleaning your house.
- *Family.* Everyone has one somewhere. They require a certain amount of time and energy. Family may be your parents, siblings, grandparents, aunts, uncles, cousins, or children. It may be friends who are more like family than your blood relatives. It's people that you give and receive support from.

Sometimes it's tempting to put these people last on your priority list, but don't. Your family needs to know that you care, and you need to be part of their lives.

- *Alone time.* This is time for you to meditate, just take a deep breath, or write in a journal. It's time for you to reflect on where you are in your life and where you're going. It may be the fifteen minutes you can steal when you take a bath, but it's important to find some time for you, even if it's only a couple of minutes.

- *Personal growth.* This is the category that includes all of those self-help, how-to books or audiotapes, seminars, and workshops you attend, or the college class you enrolled in. It's *anything* you do to help yourself grow as a person and meet goals that are important to you.

- *Career.* This is where you spend a significant number of hours each week. Make sure you enjoy what you do. Your career is a way you earn money, participate in the building of society, and develop professional skills. If you're lucky you'll feel passionate about how you earn money, but it's not your identity as a person. When you're on your deathbed you won't be thinking, "I should've spent more time at the office." Make sure this box doesn't become the one where you place all of your time, efforts, and energy. In our materialistic culture it's easy to put all of your focus here and avoid developing other areas of your life. Those other areas might be the place you find your ideal mate.

- *Significant relationship.* This is only *one* area of a whole, balanced life. It's not your whole box. Of course, you need to make time for a relationship and that special person, but they should never be your entire life. Lifelong relationships are made by two whole individuals who mutually agree to share their lives. Your significant relationship should be *a* priority, but not your only one.

- *Friends.* You should always take time to maintain old friendships and make new ones. Have you ever had friends who ditch you when a significant other shows up in their life, and then knock on your door six weeks later when the relationship didn't work out to cry on your shoulder? It's important to make sure, even when you're busy at work, with your family, or with a significant relationship, that you maintain your friendships. Good friends support you through good and bad times. Remember to nurture and cherish them.

When you're doing something, give 100 percent of yourself to that moment. If you're spending time with friends, then be there and in that moment. That means not spending all of your time complaining about what's not working in your relationship or job. When you're at work, then give it your all, but when it's time to quit and go home, leave your job at your office. Give 100 percent of yourself to whatever moment you're in. Leave the past and future exactly where they are.

If you're maintaining a whole, balanced life and if your significant-relationship box is empty, you'll feel a void, but if it's not the only thing you have in your life, that void won't feel so large and consuming. You'll still be leading a fulfilling, productive life. You'll be less likely to think it's OK to date people who don't meet your needs, just because they're a warm body. It doesn't mean the void will go away, but instead of focusing on the void you'll be participating in developing yourself as a whole person. If your whole life is about finding a mate, you become needy. If you're needy, you'll attract needy people. It's the Law of Mirroring. You must become the person you want to be with.

Some areas of your balanced-life grid will overlap. You may spend some of your leisure time with friends or family. Your company might volunteer to build a house for Habitat for Humanity. You might enjoy exercising and find that it's a way to relieve stress, so it becomes your leisure time; or you may hate exercising, so it's your personal growth project. Even after you've met your ideal mate, it's important to maintain a balanced life. If your box contains only your significant other, your personal growth will become stifled and you'll start feeling other voids in your life. Then you'll become frustrated with your relationship because it does not and cannot meet all of your needs.

At first, fitting everything in may be a challenge and feel overwhelming. Do it in small steps. As your life becomes more full and balanced, you'll have more to give to yourself and others. You'll be more in touch with your feelings and enjoying most of the moments in life. When you're enjoying yourself it's almost impossible not to be in a state of love. A balanced life is your first step to living a life based on love.

Kelly's mother and sister were visiting her over Labor Day. One evening they decided to go to an outdoor bar and listen to a band. While they were there a tall, handsome man approached Kelly and started a conversation. He introduced himself as James and said he was visiting for the weekend. Kelly, who'd recently ended a two-year relationship, asked him to join them at their table. To her surprise James took her phone number when he left.

The next day, James called and asked Kelly out for the following weekend. Kelly lived in the city and James was a rancher. Kelly didn't think this could be any more than a brief fling, so she didn't let the obvious lifestyle difference influence her decision to get to know James better. Although Kelly was independent by nature, since breaking up with her ex-boyfriend she'd been feeling a little lonely and enjoyed the attention James gave her.

The following weekend they had a great time. Kelly felt as if she'd known James all her life. For the next month he came up to the city every weekend to take her out and called her every night. The following month James started asking Kelly to join him at the ranch. Although she wasn't fond of ranches, she really liked James and wanted to spend time with him. She thought it was only fair that she do some of the commuting. At that point they began alternating weekends between his ranch and her apartment in the city.

Within four months, the arrangement had gradually evolved to her spending every weekend at the ranch. James said, "It's hard for me to travel because the cows and crops have to be taken care of every day."

James's ranch was miles away from even a grocery store. In fact, the closest town was a half-hour drive away. So they spent most of their time at the ranch. In the beginning Kelly really didn't mind, because it gave her and James a chance to be alone and really get to know each other. She was falling in love.

Of course, this meant she was spending much less time with her friends doing the things she enjoyed: hearing bands, going to the ballet, visiting art galleries, attending cultural events, watching the latest movie, and enjoying good restaurants.

James proposed once they'd been dating for six months. Kelly immediately accepted, but she recognized that she wouldn't be happy living on a ranch. When she discussed this with James, they agreed that within two years they'd move to the city and James would change careers.

Since Kelly was a sales representative for a manufacturer and worked from her home, it was easy for her to move her office to the ranch, though it meant a longer, more difficult commute to be at her appointments in the city. She thought that because of love she could survive anything, even living on a ranch for two years.

Kelly and James got married the following year. Although Kelly really wasn't happy, she thought that it was just the living on the ranch, that she was missing her friends and city life. She was hanging on to the belief that the following year they'd move.

As that year progressed she noticed James wasn't making any efforts toward moving. He hadn't started looking for a job; in fact he didn't even know what he wanted to do. Kelly's unhappiness was affecting her health; she was gaining weight and developed high blood pressure. She was depressed all the time. She and James were always fighting.

At the end of the second year she realized that James probably didn't have any intentions of moving. Though Kelly loved him and knew he loved her, she had lost her "self." She never did any of the things she enjoyed and had lost touch with most of her friends. She didn't have much in common with the other ranchers' wives, so she hadn't made new friends. Her isolation and unhappiness were taking a toll on her emotionally, physically, and spiritually.

After another year of trying to find contentment living on the ranch, Kelly moved back to the city. Although she had to go through the painful experience of divorce, she learned that a relationship couldn't be her whole life. She had to be happy as a person, happy with her life, before she could share it with someone else.

Kelly and James have remained friends. She hopes that he'll meet a nice girl from the country.

In the Name of Love

There is only one kind of love, but there are a thousand different versions.
LA ROCHEFOUCAULD

Monuments have been built, songs written, and even the English throne given up in the name of love. People have killed, stalked, and been abusive to others in the name of love. Is it any wonder that the word *love* means different things to different people?

What does love mean to you? If you grew up in a house where you received love only when you did something wonderful, kept quiet, or acted out, how did that affect your concept of love? Did your parents fight in front of you and tell you it was because they loved each other? Did they never communicate with each other because of love? Did you get lots of hugs and kisses because of love? If you believe that love was yelling, possessiveness, and lots of work, that's what you'll keep re-creating in your life. On the other hand, if you believe love is a mutually supportive partnership that enables each person to grow as a human being, then that's what you'll re-create. The key here is what you *believe*, not what you *think*. Your beliefs are imprinted in your subconscious; your subconscious creates the mirror for what you attract. If you're attracting situations and relationships that aren't compatible with what you think you want, then you need to examine your *belief system*. Most of the time your belief system was created in childhood.

The way love was verbally and nonverbally expressed in your household when you were growing up is the initial foundation for your perception of what love is and how it's lived. When you got older and began dating, you may have been told, "You'll have sex with me if you love me," "You'll do drugs with me if you love me," or, "You'll be at my beck and call twenty-four hours a day, seven days a week if you love me." You'll react to these requests or demands depending on your perception of how love is supposed to be expressed.

You may respond to your potential partner's every need, want, and concern without any consideration for your own needs if you were conditioned to believe this is the definition of love. If you're struggling to maintain your identity because you felt, as a child, as if you were emotionally drowning, you may decide never to compromise or negotiate, to the point where your obstinacy makes it difficult for others to love you.

If you're looking for your ideal mate, then it's important to know what *you* do "in the name of love." Make a list. Decide what you do that you *like*—and what you would like to *change*—about how you respond to love.

For example, if you were taught that love means not honestly communicating your feelings to your partner, then you'll attract partners who do not respond well to honest communication. Even though you may want to tell your partner how you feel, you may not be able to, because you weren't taught how or because you received a negative response in the past from being honest. You have to change your pattern of behavior. Start being honest with your friends. For example, if someone calls and wants to go to a movie that you don't want to see and normally you'd either go and say nothing or make up an excuse, try saying, "I really don't like violent movies, but thanks for calling. I hear X is good; could we see that instead?" Eventually you'll apply this principle in other areas of your life, including your significant relationships.

On the other hand, what about the messages about love you received that you liked? Did you always kiss your parents good night? Were you taught to give your friends and family loving hugs? Did your mother bake your favorite cookies if she thought you had a bad day? If you've had positive experiences about expressing love that you want to re-create, then do that.

If you're living in a state of love, it doesn't mean doing things that are loving only toward people that you're romantically attracted to. It means practicing the Golden Rule, "Do unto others as you'd have others do unto you." This doesn't mean just select others; it means humankind in general. Are you kind and considerate to your friends? If someone has been ill, do you offer to bring over chicken soup? If someone is having a down moment, do you offer a nonjudgmental ear for listening? Do you celebrate the successes of your friends and family? Can you be genuinely happy for people when their lives are going well? *Or* are you kinder to strangers than you are to your own friends and family? Do you continually offer unsolicited advice? Do you try to control other people's actions and behaviors, either overtly or covertly? Are you envious of other people's good fortunes?

My point is, how do you act toward others in the name of love? If you aren't loving toward people you're involved with in a nonromantic way, then it'll be next to impossible to be living in a state of love with a romantic partner.

Love means different things to different people. Because we all have different ideals about what love is and isn't, our expectations, actions, and responses to it are different. Some people say women are more open to giving and receiving love than men. I disagree. I believe that everyone has felt pain in the name of love. If we've ever felt pain, we'll try to avoid a repeat experience of it at all costs. This means that at some point most of us will build a fence around our heart to protect it from the possible pain associated with love. Different people will build different kinds of fences. Some fences are of solid rock, without a gate or a window. Others are just chain-link fences with plenty of gates for people of the owner's choosing to enter and exit. Some people have locked their gates and thrown away the keys, and some have fences of string, allowing everyone, including people who shouldn't have access, to enter. Fortunately, it's *your* fence—and you can tear down your rock fence, or change guards, or toughen the entry requirements. You built your protective fence based on your ideas, perceptions, and experiences of love.

In the name of love you can remodel it, tear it down, or find the keys to unlock the gate.

Having a security fence around your foundation of love means having healthy boundaries. It's not selfish; it's about loving yourself first.

Self-Love Versus Selfish

Selfishness is not living as one wishes to live, it is asking others
to live as one wishes to live.
OSCAR WILDE

When you're practicing self-love by taking care of yourself, others may call you selfish because you're not at the mercy of their agenda. It's important to recognize the difference between self-love and being selfish.

Self-love is about accepting the responsibility of taking care of your physical, emotional, mental, and spiritual needs. It's about recognizing that if you don't take care of yourself, you aren't in a position to give love—or anything else—to others. Practicing self-love is recognizing the needs of your body and respecting them. It is choosing to stay home and watch a movie instead of going out partying with friends if you're ill or tired.

Selfishness, on the other hand, is about wanting what's best for yourself without regard to what's best for others. It means that your motives, actions, and interactions with others are based only on self-serving goals. For example: someone you like calls you, you're not home, they leave a message, and you choose not to call them back, because you want them to chase you. You have a self-serving motive for your actions. This isn't a kind, loving action. Would you want someone you liked not to call *you* back because they wanted you to call them more? Would *you* want to call someone more when they aren't even courteous enough to return your phone call?

Unfortunately, when you're practicing self-love it's often perceived by others as selfishness. If you're ever accused of this or anything else, I suggest that you do two things: First, consider the source; if it's reliable, look at the issue. Second, remember that the accuser may need to look at their own life with a mirror instead of looking at yours with a magnifying glass. When you've chosen to live your life by spiritual principles, there's always a tendency to struggle with the "unconditional love" philosophy. You may even feel that by practicing self-love you aren't loving others unconditionally. But self-love is about *first* loving yourself unconditionally so that you can mirror that to the world. That means having healthy boundaries.

Healthy boundaries are a part of unconditional love. When you have healthy boundaries you know what works and doesn't work in your life; you know what you like and don't like in the people you associate with and the lifestyle you have. Some people like to party until 4 A.M. and others like to have sweet dreams at that hour. Some like being outdoors, swimming and playing softball, while others prefer going to movies, museums, and the theater. It's not that something's wrong with liking one thing and not the other, or that people with diversified interests can't happily bond, but it's about knowing what does and doesn't fit in your life. Of course, some boundaries are about keeping out things that hurt us. If someone is abusive verbally or physically, is not supportive of your goals and dreams, or doesn't make you feel good about yourself, then keeping such a person out of your life is about protecting yourself from harm.

Unconditional love means not putting conditions upon love, and that means not judging others. Native American philosophy teaches "Never judge someone until you've walked in their moccasins." Unconditional love allows others to live their own lives and learn their lessons when they're ready. It's trusting that when the student is ready, the teacher will appear, and recognizing and accepting that you may not be everyone's teacher. This means that you may have to love people from afar. Your goal is to have loving thoughts toward everyone, even those you feel did you wrong. However, you may decide someone shouldn't be part of your everyday life. Living in a state of love doesn't mean being a martyr. So, if you love someone who's abusive to you, I'm not suggesting you should stop loving them. God knows they need all the love they can get. I am saying that you need to have a boundary about what role they play in your life. If someone verbally attacks you, then I wouldn't invite them over for dinner just because I was trying to live in a state of love. Invite someone over who's also trying to live in a state of love, and you'll actually enjoy the evening.

Self-love isn't selfish. It's about taking care of yourself, which will give you the energy, patience, and tolerance to actually love others unconditionally.

Rob and Jill had been dating since Jill was fifteen. Rob had wanted to get married from the moment Jill turned eighteen, but Jill didn't feel she was ready.

Jill accepted Rob's proposal when she turned twenty. Within twenty-four hours of putting the engagement ring on her finger, she had welts all over her hand.

"My whole ring finger swelled up, and it turned into a rash," Jill said. "It was very obvious that I didn't want to get married. My finger was red hot. All I could think was, 'I've got to get this ring off my hand.'"

She went to the beach with her girlfriends, and her hand hurt so much that all she wanted to do was fling off the ring. It was a one-carat-diamond ring, hardly the kind of jewelry you'd just throw off at the beach. But Jill said, "I couldn't stand it, so I flung the ring off into the sand.

"The moment I took it off, I was instantaneously relieved," Jill said. She felt her body was obviously recognizing that she was uncomfortable with the idea of being engaged, much less married.

She told Rob that night that this wasn't right for her and she probably wouldn't be ready to get married anytime soon. She felt bad because the relationship had been progressing in the direction of marriage but she hadn't told him that she wasn't comfortable with it.

That experience taught her how important it was to her physical well-being to be in touch with how she was feeling about a situation and how important it was to express it.

Types of Love

We are shaped and fashioned by what we love.
GOETHE

I believe that there are five types of love in relationships: physical, spiritual, mental, emotional, and holistic. It's very possible to have only one of the first four types of love with someone. You may love the mental stimulation you have when you're communicating with someone but not be physically attracted to them. You may be physically attracted to someone but have no other love connections. You may even have a spiritual connection with someone and loving feelings toward them but, again, be lacking in other love connections. For a relationship with a lifetime ideal mate to work—to have a holistic relationship—you must connect on *all* levels.

Physical love is sexual. It's the unexplainable chemistry and attraction you have for someone. Some of us are sexually attracted to a specific body type, hair or eye color, or something that we just can't define. Physical chemistry with someone usually doesn't develop over time. But as you become more comfortable with a person spiritually, mentally, and emotionally, you may recognize your feelings and allow repressed or denied physical chemistry to finally ignite. However, if you considered a person unappealing when you met, it's unlikely you'll feel sexual chemistry even if you love and adore them on all of the other levels.

Physical love is also about the compatibility of how love is expressed. Some of us are Victoria's Secret romantics, while others prefer the excitement of leather, handcuffs, and blindfolds. Some people like role-playing, others may want multiple partners, and some want candlelight, romantic music, and rose petals in bed. The point is to know how you think physical love should be expressed and to develop your boundaries around what you are comfortable with. Keep in mind that as relationships grow and change, your ideas about the expression of physical love may also change.

In the beginning most relationships are based on physical attraction. This attraction may be expressed through kisses, hugs, holding hands, or making love. But regardless of how you choose to express your physical love for someone, it's important to remember that you need to develop all types of love and not get stuck in the expression of just physical love.

Spiritual love is divine, nonsexual, cosmic, unconditional, and all-encompassing. When you look in someone's eyes, it may feel as if you've known them forever. You're kindred spirits. At a soul level you want what's best for the other person. It's like the love a mother has for a child or a child has for a parent. Regardless of what the other person does, you'll always love them, even if you don't like their actions. Spiritual love involves recognizing that you can't control or manipulate the journey of another person. It's trusting and having faith that all things happen as they should, even if you don't understand or like it. Spiritual love allows people to spread their wings and fly.

You also need to be compatible regarding how you think spirituality should be expressed. Spirituality is how you relate to God, or the universal forces. If you believe spirituality is going to church or synagogue every week and your potential partner doesn't even believe in God, or you think all you need to do is meditate to talk to God and you're dating someone who wants to be a minister, then you'll have to do some negotiating to find common ground about spiritual expression.

Mental love is the intellectual stimulation that you get when you're communicating with another. It gives the relationship the energy and passion that motivates you to think. Maybe the other person can offer you insights about yourself that others haven't been able to see; maybe they teach you things you've always wanted to know about; or perhaps they just plant seeds of wisdom and you harvest them. In a significant relationship there should be a mutual mental love and admiration for each other. You have expertise in different areas, but when you're sharing there should be a mental bond that is mutually energetic.

Relationships can be based on many different mental stimulations. Maybe you each have a passion for the arts, your careers, or saving the whales. You don't have to be intellectual equals, but you do need to share in certain interests that you can learn about and explore together.

Emotional love involves the intense feelings another person can bring up. This encompasses all feelings, both positive and negative. You may feel love and hate, joy and sadness, or serenity and pain all in the same conversation with someone. A person you love emotionally will have the ability to put you on cloud nine—or pull the cord that sends you falling and hitting the cement faster than you can read this sentence. When you love someone emotionally you open a door to vulnerability. When they feel hurt, you'll feel hurt; when they're happy, you're happy. Of course, unless emotional love is mutual, this can be a very draining kind of love. If you're emotionally connected to someone and the feeling isn't reciprocated, then you're vulnerable to their hurting you, either accidentally or intentionally. They may not realize their responses or actions have a large impact on you. Of course, when the feeling is mutual, both partners try to be emotionally supportive and considerate. This allows people to feel emotionally safe and secure, so love can blossom and grow for both of them. As your emotional love grows it will allow you to take risks that you may have been too afraid to take in the past.

Emotional love should be given with appropriate boundaries in order to prevent unnecessary emotional damage. You need to take emotional risks, but it may be wise to have a safety net in place or not to jump until you're sure that you'll be landing on something soft and secure. If in the past you were hurt by emotional love, you may need to practice it in small increments. You may start with allowing yourself to be emotionally vulnerable with your friends. Once you're secure with those relationships, you'll be able to move into emotional vulnerability with a romantic partner.

Holistic love in a relationship encompasses love at the physical, mental, emotional, and spiritual levels. This allows for the most growth as individuals, therefore paving the path for infinite relationship growth. If your relationship can't experience love on the physical, mental, spiritual, and emotional planes simultaneously, you'll end up feeling a void and trying to fill it elsewhere. There may be times that your relationship is experiencing growth in one area more than another, but there's still a balance. Holistic love is a necessary foundation for a lifelong loving relationship.

During your journey to finding your ideal mate, you may meet romantic partners with whom you bond in only one or two areas. This allows you to grow in a particular area of your life by finding out what you want and don't want in a relationship. For example, you may meet someone and have a mental bond. You can talk for hours. This relationship may have been about realizing that someone can appreciate your thoughts and ideas. You may find out that you can share interests that are intellectually stimulating. However, the physical chemistry or other bonds might not be strong enough for a holistic relationship. This doesn't mean that you didn't learn about yourself and grow as a person or that the relationship wasn't a critical part of the experiences that will take you to your ideal mate.

Preparing yourself for a holistic relationship with your ideal mate involves understanding your physical, spiritual, emotional, and mental love needs and wants. It's about allowing yourself to love others on all those levels. It's recognizing that all relationships you experience are opportunities to learn to love someone physically, emotionally, spiritually, and mentally. In time, with practice, you'll find yourself in a state of holistic love.

Faith, Trust, and Release

In real love you want the other person's good.
In romantic love you want the other person.
MARGARET ANDERSON

If you love something, set it free. If it comes back to you, it is yours.
If it doesn't, it never was.
ANONYMOUS

Living in a state of love requires that you have faith and trust in a higher, universal order to life. It's having faith and trusting that when you love others—even if that love isn't returned in the way you expect or want it to be returned—you're living an experience that's of the highest good for your soul's growth. It requires releasing expectations. When you expect people to act or react to the love you give them, then it's love with strings attached. Love with strings is more about power and ego than about living in love.

When you give in an attempt to receive, you alter the flow of loving energy. Giving love isn't like going shopping and giving the salesclerk money in exchange for an item you picked out to meet your needs; the laws of the universe don't work like the laws of consumerism. You can't decide exactly what you get in return for the love you give others. Real love is about releasing all expectations for what you get in return, while maintaining faith and trust that you're practicing your soul's highest purpose, the purpose of loving others. Universal law does allow for you to receive tenfold anything given without expectations; it just doesn't specify what, when, and how you receive.

Living in a state of love means you have faith and trust that even though you don't know the outcome of the love you give, the experience is in your best interest. This is hard, especially when you feel you're giving out more love than you're receiving. It may help to become more aware of all the love that you receive. Sometimes it may feel as if you're looking for a needle in a haystack, but you must count your blessings. Keeping a gratitude journal or list may help remind you of the loving things that come into your life.

If you aren't receiving love back in the way you express it or want it expressed to you, examine your definition of love and how you believe love should be expressed. You may need to strengthen your boundaries. That doesn't mean building a fence that doesn't have a key or a gate, but it may mean being more discerning about how you express love. Living in a state of love isn't about hurting yourself. So, if someone doesn't return your affections and efforts to show them love, you shouldn't keep trying to be part of their life in an attempt to live in a state of love. You should release them and send loving thoughts; you should let go of your willingness to have people who don't reciprocate your feelings and actions in a healthy way actively participate in your life. They don't have to be in love with you, but they can still be kind and considerate of your feelings.

The principle of faith, trust, and release is one of the hardest to practice. It's asking yourself to separate from your ego and allow your spiritual nature to be in charge. This is difficult to do when we live in a culture that emphasizes who's right and who's wrong. You must make a conscious choice every day to live in a state of love while practicing faith, trust, and release. Some days you may have to make the choice moment by moment, especially if you're in the middle of those Murphy's Law times in your life when nothing seems to be going right. You have to practice faith, trust, and release not only with relationships but in all areas of your life.

Of course, some people will take practicing faith, trust, and release to the extreme. Practicing faith, trust, and release doesn't replace action and effort. Living in a state of love means that you take care of yourself, which includes setting goals, loving your fellow man, and putting forth the necessary efforts to get what you want, but ultimately releasing your expectations and having faith and trust that all experiences are a part of God's plan for you.

Gwen met her first husband, Tony, when she was in college. He played football and she was a cheerleader. They got married, had two children, and Tony began playing professional football after college. The lifestyle of a professional football player didn't fit well with Gwen's ideal life. She saw her husband change from the person she married to someone she really didn't know. Gwen said, "He started believing his own press releases."

Gwen was very interested in working with the body to stop the aging process. When she wanted to start her own business, her husband responded, "I don't need a wife that works; I need someone who'll totally dedicate their life to me."

This was a turning point; after twelve years of marriage, Gwen decided to leave. She became very project focused and was pursuing her life's work: body work.

She also decided she was going to have fun, so she dated a lot. One November evening at a local bar, Gwen saw Bob beating the bar ledge and dancing. She walked up to him and said, "If you've got that much energy, then you can certainly channel it in a much better way."

They talked and Gwen gave Bob her business card. He said he'd call.

Bob lost his wallet with Gwen's business card in it. After about six weeks he was concerned because he didn't want her thinking that he said he was going to do something and didn't. He remembered the name of her street and that she drove a Jeep with an out-of-state license plate. He drove up and down the street and found what he thought was her car. She and the girlfriend she was living with were walking out to go to dinner at the exact moment he pulled up.

Gwen says, "You have to respect the unexplainable. He hunted me down and found me."

They quickly became friends and started doing everything together. Neither of them had any plans to ever get remarried. Gwen had found the playmate she was looking for.

Gwen was out of state on a trip and got a call one day telling her that Bob had been shot while someone was trying to rob him at his store. Gwen's first thought was, "I don't want him to die." At that moment she realized that she cared deeply for Bob.

Gwen helped nurse Bob back to health. In April they moved in together, and by September they were married. They've been married for fifteen years. Gwen was looking for a friend and found one in Bob. Friends allow each other to be themselves; they help and support each other. She and Bob are play-mates for life.

Gwen knew exactly what she wanted in a mate but let God choose the package. She was open to whoever that man turned out to be. In fact, Gwen and Bob are an interracial couple.

Gwen realizes the accident was the very catalyst that made her aware of how strong her feelings were. Sometimes life hands you a strange deck of cards and it's up to you how you play them.

Random Acts of Kindness

Wherever there is a human being there is an opportunity for kindness.
SENECA

One of the best ways to express your love to others is to practice random acts of kindness. Random acts of kindness are exactly that— kind things you randomly decide to do without expecting anything in return. This means you may be a good Samaritan and not even be acknowledged or thanked. The person who was the beneficiary of your good deed may not even know you were their secret angel.

Some sample random acts of kindness are

- opening a door for someone
- smiling at strangers on the street
- calling or going to visit someone who's been ill or down in the dumps
- paying someone a compliment
- leaving flowers on someone's desk at work
- throwing your neighbor's newspaper closer to their door
- allowing a car on the highway to move into your lane

You may think these things are simple or that anyone can do them. You're right, they are. How many random acts of kindness do you commit a day? Each time you make a kind, loving gesture without any expectation attached, you are living in a state of love. A random act of kindness doesn't have to cost money or require plans. It's recognizing a moment that you can do something nice for someone else and taking advantage of it.

If we feel that our lives aren't like we'd like them to be, or if we hurt emotionally, one of the best ways to feel the energy of love is to help someone else. Everyone will have times when they're in the middle of one of life's rainstorms: you broke up with the love of your life, your boss isn't being nice, or you're spending lots of unexpected money on something unplanned, like car repairs. But even when you're feeling low there's someone else who needs a kind word, a smile, or a hug just as much as you could benefit from giving it. Ultimately, when you give, it puts you in a place where you can receive.

When we're doing loving things without expectations, we're experiencing love at that moment. Practicing random acts of kindness gives you the opportunity to live in love, if only for small moments at a time. But every moment adds up. Eventually, when you're practicing random acts of kindness out of habit, who knows how many moments of love you'll be living in effortlessly?

Jappy, who lives in Fort Lauderdale, shares her story in her own words.

Freddy and I were the best of friends. He was almost my stepson because his father and I were engaged to be married, but sadly his father passed away three months before the wedding was to take place. One night Freddy and I were having dinner. I noticed he looked down.

I asked, "What's the matter?"

He responded, "The lack of girls, especially ones who play golf."

Freddy loves golf and is a fine golfer. We put our heads together and decided to start a club called Golf Lovers. It was quite a success. We ended up with about eighty members, both men and women, and ten golf clubs participated.

Once it was started I got out because I didn't play golf and worked every day. But Freddy continued it.

Meanwhile a man named Bill Ryan, who'd lost his wife a year before and had just moved to Fort Lauderdale, saw the *Golf Lovers* ad in the paper. He called Freddy and joined the club. He loved it. As soon as Freddy met him, he decided that he had other plans for Bill than just *Golf Lovers*.

Freddy suggested that Bill give me a call, so he gave him my work phone number. I didn't have a clue I was being fixed up. Instead of calling me, Bill came to call on me at the shop where I worked. It was a rainy day and he arrived with one long-stem red rose in his hand. He introduced himself. I was so surprised. He seemed like a nice fellow, so we went to dinner the following week. He was tall, lanky, and bashful. Things just took off from there, and within four months we were married.

When we met for our first date, he brought me a present. He's the old-fashioned type who still does sweet things.

We've been married for four years now, all because of *Golf Lovers*. Ironically, Freddy, for whom the club was founded, has yet to find the girl of his dreams.

The Art of Receiving

Love is but the discovery of ourselves in others,
and the delight in the recognition.
ALEXANDER SMITH

When you're living in a state of love you must be able to give love to yourself and others, but it's equally important to be able to receive it. It's the Law of Mirroring. Giving is necessary, but it's only half of the equation. If you don't know how to receive love from others, it'll be impossible to form a mutually loving relationship. You'll be doing all of the giving and eventually get resentful and angry that you aren't getting anything back in return for your energy and efforts. A simple way to gauge how you receive love is to evaluate your reaction when someone gives you a compliment. For example, if someone says, "You look good in that dress," what's your response? Do you say, "Thank you," and feel good about yourself for a moment? Or do you respond, "Oh, this old thing," and act as if you have to apologize for looking good?

The art of receiving is something that we don't know how to do very well. There isn't great precedent for it or many role models to learn from. There's a fear of just saying "Thank you" for a compliment, because we might appear egotistical. If someone gives us a gift that's either material or takes time, then we may wonder, "What do they want?" or, "Do I deserve it?" In either case it's difficult for us to just receive in grace. Women have a difficult time receiving because we've been taught from birth by society that we are the givers and nurturers. However, men have an equally difficult time receiving because they feel that receiving isn't manly or the giver wants something back in return. Neither experience is any easier to work through; they're just different.

Are you able to receive acts of kindness from others? Don't forget that acts of kindness aren't things done for you that you expect to be done by someone you love. They're kind acts done spontaneously by anyone—including family, friends, lovers, coworkers, neighbors, and even strangers. Do you recognize when loving acts are being done on your behalf? How do you react if someone does something nice for you? For example, if a friend sends you a plant, do you respond by feeling obligated to send them something in return, or do you feel grateful that you have a friend who loves you enough to take the time to brighten your day?

Remember, real loving acts are things done without any expectations. So, if the people who claim that they're doing loving acts for you are expecting a specific response or behavior in exchange, then it's not real love being expressed. It's an action in exchange for a reaction.

However, loving thoughts and acts may come your way from total strangers. Kind words and deeds may be done by people that you barely know. Accept them at face value. Think of any kind gestures as gifts of love from the Universe.

If you have trouble allowing loving thoughts and gestures into your life, start off slow. Learn how to accept compliments. As you learn how to accept the loving gestures and thoughts of others, your mirror of giving and receiving will begin to flow. You won't feel as if you're giving more than you receive, because you'll recognize the countless times a day when you have the opportunity to receive love.

Many times people feel that they give more than they receive. And often they *do*, because they don't know how to accept love or they think it has to come back to them in a specific way. For example, if someone cooks dinner for their significant other, they may expect the loving act to be returned by that person taking them out to dinner the next week. In reality, the return for that loving act may come in the form of someone else taking them to dinner, or a stranger doing a kind deed for them, or just the opportunity to enjoy the company of their significant other. My point is, you can't have an attachment to how you expect the loving act to be returned.

Attachments to outcomes block the flow of energy, so when you're giving and receiving love, don't expect any specific outcome. The Universe will send you treasures that are beyond your highest expectations. However, to find the treasure you must let go of expectations and learn to allow yourself to receive the gifts given to you.

Living in Love

*To love for the sake of being loved is human, but to love
for the sake of loving is angelic.*
ALPHONSE DE LAMARTINE

Living in a state of love is the most rewarding and challenging experience you'll ever have. Living in love allows you to feel great joys, find serenity, and have faith in the order of life. Unfortunately, it's also the door for pain, disappointment, and fear.

Love can heal all things, but the healing may occur in a form that you never expected. Love recognizes that it's the bonding force of life. It doesn't recognize expectations. In fact, it'll go out of its way to force you to see beyond your limitations. Love isn't in a box. It's a circle that encompasses everyone and all experiences.

Loving someone will not change them unless they're ready to change. When people change, it's an internal job. Love can provide a safe place for people to choose to grow and improve their lives, but *they* must make that choice and do the work. However, when you allow yourself to unconditionally love someone, it can change you. It opens your heart so you can give and receive love. When you love someone, it's about allowing yourself to experience the highest vibration we can as human beings.

When we're practicing living in love it opens the doors for miracles to happen. Of course, miracles are God-given gifts, and with any gift there can't be expectations, only gratitude for the experience.

Gene had spent the past four months affirming the qualities he wanted in an ideal mate. He wanted to meet someone who was attractive, loving, good-hearted, and extremely affectionate. Gene realized it wasn't so much about what the person was like as about how he felt when he was with that person. He believed that his mate was out there; it was just a matter of when he would find her. He sent his request to God and trusted that everything happens as it should.

Helen had been preparing to meet her ideal mate for the past year. She was actively writing down the traits she wanted to attract, releasing old fears, healing wounds, meditating to send out love, and releasing worries about who would come into her life. She was busy living her life, enjoying it, and following her intuition.

Helen was picking up a friend at a local cultural center, which was hosting an evening of flute music. Gene had been drawn there that night to hear the music. Helen and Gene had passed in the hallway, but it wasn't until after the performance that they ended up in the same room with each other alone. Helen was waiting for her friend, and Gene was enjoying his relaxed meditative state.

Helen and Gene started talking to each other in silly British accents and began playing. They immediately recognized the good energy between them. Gene asked for Helen's phone number and eagerly waited twenty-four hours to call.

They hit it off and began seeing each other every day. Although Gene was forty-five and Helen was forty-four, neither one had ever been married. They had both previously had long-term committed relationships, but neither felt intuitively led to marry. But in this relationship they felt as if they were being reunited. It was natural and flowing. Within seven months they were living together, and they have been engaged for a year. They feel married but they just haven't set the date for the party.

Although Helen and Gene have differences, those differences don't harm the relationship, so they respect them and don't try to change them. Gene and Helen balance and complement each other. They never fight, but that doesn't mean they don't have spirited conversations. Both of them recognize the importance of being individuals.

Helen and Gene believe they have been able to come together because they were content and happy with themselves before they met. They weren't looking for someone to complete them, but to share with them. "It's not that you're creating a mate; you're merely identifying who it is," says Gene.

Artists, poets, writers, musicians, and philosophers have all been trying to describe and understand love since the beginning of time. Love is something that we experience at a soul level. It's something that transcends all other emotions. Living in love frees us to be kind to ourselves and our fellow man. It's the highest form of energy that can resonate from your being.

Everyone has access to an infinite supply of love available to them. It's something that's self-generated. The more loving we are to ourselves and others, the more love we're able to receive. Yet ironically, love is something that we tend to give others as if it were in scarce supply. It's as if we fear we'll run out and won't have any more to give. Granted, giving love increases your vulnerability and your risk of feeling hurt, pain, and disappointment. But without love you also experience hurt, pain, and disappointment. These emotions are part of being human, and without experiencing them, you wouldn't have a concept of how beautiful it is to experience joy, happiness, and peace. Living a life full of love is the greatest challenge and accomplishment you can achieve. Love doesn't shelter you from experiencing pain and sorrow; it's the fuel that allows you to soar through life, ultimately transcending them, to experience great happiness, joy, faith, and trust.

There is only one happiness in life, to love and be loved.

GEORGE SAND

Love is patient and kind; love is not jealous or boastful; it is not arrogant or rude. Love doesn't insist on its own way; it is not irritable or resentful; it does not rejoice at wrong, but rejoices in the right. Love bears all things, believes all things, hopes all things, endures all things.

I CORINTHIANS 13:4–7

Part Two

Law of Preparation and Attraction

Destiny is not a matter of chance; it is a matter of choice. It is not a thing to be waited for; it is a thing to be achieved.
WILLIAM JENNINGS BRYAN

What we are today comes from our thoughts of yesterday, and our present thoughts build our life of tomorrow: Our life is a creation of our mind.
THE BUDDHA

I wish I could write a foolproof guide to the metaphysical principles of the Law of Preparation and Attraction so you could create the perfect life and you wouldn't have to go through any aggravation, pain, or suffering. However, experiences that we would rather avoid are just as important to the growth of our soul as experiencing joy, happiness, and love. During your journey you'll meet people who don't mirror the positive qualities you're trying to project. Despite your best efforts and intentions, people who are manipulative, self-serving, and angry will be part of your reality. In some cases, you'll be able to recognize them and say, "No, thank you." In other cases they may be in your life so that you can learn patience, tolerance, and acceptance. They may be people you work with, members of your family, or even your own children. The point is that despite all your best efforts to prepare and attract positive experiences, some bad ones will still happen. And how you perceive life and the challenges it offers will determine how you react to unpleasant experiences.

Pretend that all negative experiences are mosquitoes. If you're going to go outside, you'll have to contend with these annoying insects, and despite your best intentions, you may not be able to avoid them. They're waiting for someone to walk into their airspace so they can land on them and feast on their blood. You have a choice: you walk into mosquito land unprepared and become a target for multiple bites; or you prepare for your outing by wearing long sleeves, using some type of insect repellent; or you avoid going out at dawn and dusk, when they're out in full force. During certain times of the year, you just can't avoid them, no matter how positively you think, how much you visualize, or how many affirmations you state. It's your *preparation* for them that determines how much they'll affect your life. In some cases, you may avoid being bitten altogether; other times you may get only a bite or two; or if you aren't prepared, you can get so many bites that you feel like you have the chicken pox. The point is that negative people and experiences *do* exist, and from time to time they'll affect your life despite your best efforts to avoid them. You can *choose* how you react to those experiences.

Although we will all be confronted with negative people and experiences, I have to state that I *do* believe we have the ability to manifest things into our life. We can manifest both positive and negative experiences. If you're putting more of your energy into creating positive situations, you'll attract more positive experiences than negative ones. However, if all of your energy and efforts are put into negative or fear-based thoughts, you'll create more of those situations. One of my colleagues gave me this analogy that explains the concept of focusing: When you take snow-skiing or Rollerblading lessons, you're told that your body will adjust to where your eyes are looking. For example, when you're skiing, if your eyes fixate on a tree in front of you, your body will automatically adjust itself and head right into the tree. You would never intentionally *try* to ski into a tree; in fact, consciously you'd make every effort to avoid it. But lots of skiers end up with broken legs or other injuries because they crashed into trees. The point is, whatever you're focusing on with your eyes, energy, and attention, you'll naturally gravitate toward with seemingly no effort. In fact, you might even end up creating a situation that you ordinarily would try to consciously avoid simply because you spend so much time fearing that it will happen.

Consider the ski analogy when you think about relationships. How often are we focusing on what could go wrong? Eventually, when something does go wrong, we say, "You see, I was right; that was a real jerk." Of course, this can actually *be* the case from time to time, but is it *always?* By focusing on what could go wrong, did you in effect set the wheels of universal law into action and actually create it?

Practicing the Law of Preparation and Attraction requires work and commitment. Preparing for and attracting your ideal mate is a lot like homemade desserts. For example, most people love homemade cheesecake, but they rarely, if ever, take the time to buy the ingredients and prepare it. It takes several hours to make the crust, mix the ingredients, and bake them. Then you have to let your cheesecake cool before you can taste it. But the reward for all your efforts is a piece of cake that melts in your mouth. Most of us don't prioritize the time to make homemade cheesecake, even though we prefer it to the ones we buy at a supermarket or a restaurant, so when we're craving homemade cheesecake, we usually settle for one that's bought. Unfortunately, a relationship with your ideal mate can't be bought at a supermarket or restaurant just because you're willing to settle for that and you don't want to put the effort into *creating* one.

In order to attract your ideal mate you must first prepare yourself for the experience. This means cleaning out your emotional suitcase, healing old wounds, deciding exactly what you want in a relationship, and living in love. It won't happen overnight. You may have to go through several relationships to work through emotional issues, heal old wounds, or figure out exactly what does and doesn't work for you in a relationship. Preparation involves becoming like the person you would want to be with. It's applying the Law of Mirroring. It's learning to let go, living in love and listening to and following your intuition.

Next, put effort into things that help you attract your ideal mate. This includes visualization, affirmations, meditation, creating a goal board, hypnotherapy, angelic assistance, praying, and actually putting yourself in situations where you can meet new people. You can't just wish and hope to find a mate; you have to put effort into it.

Also, you can't set your sights on a specific person and then decide that person is who you're going to prepare for and attract into your life. The Universe gave everyone free will so they can pick and choose where they want to be and with whom. There aren't any metaphysical principles that enable you to supersede another person's free will. Preparing yourself for a relationship may create an opportunity for a relationship with a specific someone to develop, but it may also allow you to move past that person and into a mutually fulfilling relationship with someone else.

Again, as I said in the beginning, there isn't a foolproof way to prepare for and attract a lifetime mate. Relationships are as unique as the two people involved. Creating the ideal relationship isn't like building your ideal house with a proven method for actually constructing the house, where you can design a blueprint, pick and choose all of the features you want, and call a builder. Healthy relationships involve two people, each on an individual journey, who mutually agree to come together to grow and share their lives. There'll be perfect moments, but each relationship will have moments of growth that aren't comfortable. Remember when you were a kid and you started losing your baby teeth? They'd get loose and eventually fall out or get pulled. Your reward for the pain was when the tooth fairy came to give you money for the baby tooth. Then you'd have to experience the discomfort and pain of cutting your permanent teeth. Of course, with proper dental hygiene, your permanent teeth will last a lifetime, so the discomfort is definitely worth the outcome. A relationship with your ideal mate can be the same way. Although there will be times of discomfort, in the end the rewards far outweigh it.

Law of Preparation

Plan ahead; it wasn't raining when Noah built the ark.
ANONYMOUS

Listening to your heart is not simple. Finding out who you are is not simple.
It takes a lot of hard work and courage to get to know
who you are and what you want.
SUE BENDER

Preparation is rarely easy and never beautiful.
MAYA ANGELOU

Applying the Law of Preparation requires taking an intense, honest inventory of yourself and your ideas about relationships, and then being willing to make changes. It can be a difficult and draining experience, but it can also open the door that allows you to receive great rewards. Preparation is about getting to know yourself and welcoming growth. One of the few things guaranteed in life is change. The only question is how you respond. Do you choose to fight it, or grow from it? Relationships are one of the best opportunities for us to learn about ourselves and to grow. But growth is always easier if we've done our best to prepare for the journey.

Think of looking for your ideal mate the same way you would plan a trip. Sometimes it's fun to hop in your car and just drive, exploring new places without any game plan about your destination, but this isn't the best way to travel if you know exactly where you want to go. If you know you want to travel from Miami to Denver, you'll probably get there quicker, on better roads, and with less hassle if you look at a map before leaving. When you want to attract a life mate, you definitely have a destination in mind, so the more preparation you do, the easier the journey will be. When you're going from Miami to Denver, you may want to see a few sights along the way; you'll need to stay in hotels, and you'll need various clothes for the different climates. If you plan the trip you can make reservations and decide where you want to visit, and you'll know what to pack. It doesn't mean that you won't get lost, won't need something you didn't pack, or won't have to make other adjustments along the way; but a trip with a planned destination is always a lot easier if you've done a little preparation before you leave.

Making preparations to meet your ideal mate isn't always as easy as planning a trip. It can provide you an itinerary for what you'd like to accomplish, but you still have to be open and willing to adjust your plans as new people and experiences become part of your life. Even so, if you've prepared yourself, you'll have the inner resources and tools to make the necessary adjustments to life's little surprises.

Law of Mirroring

*Stop trying to figure out why someone acts the way he or she does. The powerful
question is: "Why do I react the way I do?"*
SUSAN JEFFERS

*I have learned silence from the talkative, tolerance from the intolerant, and
kindness from the unkind. I should not be ungrateful to those teachers.*
KAHLIL GIBRAN

The theory behind the Law of Mirroring is that the people and situations in your life are a direct reflection of your own attitudes, fears, and ideas. For example, if you continually attract angry people—your significant other, friends, or even just someone in line at the grocery store—then the mirror would be your own anger issues. Maybe you suppress or control your anger, but it's still there. If you have a fear of being alone, you'll attract others who have the same fear. If your relationship pattern is to be involved with people who seem to lack commitment, then the mirror would be your own commitment issues.

When you apply the Law of Mirroring, you have to be able to detach from situations that evoke emotions you don't like. When you're angry or upset with a person or situation, "Pick up the mirror instead of the magnifying glass," says Dr. Susan Jeffers. Usually the person or the situation is reflecting back to you an issue you need to work on, and that's the reason for your powerful emotional response. Looking at the mirror (instead of at the other person with a magnifying glass) doesn't mean you're supposed to blame yourself for the situation; it means that you become empowered to make changes and move beyond the situation. Learning to recognize mirrors isn't about fixing or changing the other person; it's about *your* growth, which then opens the door for you to create the life you want.

Have you ever dated someone that you really liked, but felt afraid to share how you felt? If so, then the other person was probably afraid to tell *you* something, too. When you're in a relationship, the mere fact that you become aware of what the mirror might be doesn't mean that you should announce what you think you're mirroring. It may be more appropriate to spend some time visualizing yourself telling the other person that you really like them. Let yourself become comfortable with the idea of sharing your feelings before you actually share them. As you begin to work through your fear, the other person may be mirroring *that,* too. Eventually, when it feels right, you'll have an opportunity to express your feelings.

Sometimes it's difficult to recognize what the mirror is in a relationship. You may think that you're ready for and want a permanent relationship, but when you attract someone who doesn't want a permanent relationship, you think there can't possibly be a mirror in this situation. However, if you take a deep look at your *real beliefs,* not just what you *want* or *think* about relationships, you may find that you *believe* you'll get hurt or be left, or that the relationship won't work out anyway. Maybe you have every reason to fear these things, based on past experiences, but if you *believe* the relationship that you want will not happen, you'll attract only people who will ensure that belief becomes a reality.

The Law of Mirroring can't be deceived by what we *claim* we believe. It's like looking in a mirror of truth. It reflects our best and worst traits, fears and hopes, and highest and lowest moments. When we meet people and can recognize the mirror, it's a gift from the Universe. It's an opportunity to learn, make changes, and grow.

The challenge when applying the Law of Mirroring is to avoid becoming too self-analyzing and critical. If you're analyzing every moment of your life, you can actually suffer from "paralysis by analysis." You aren't *living* your life, just analyzing it. For instance, if you meet someone who is abusive to you, the mirror may not have to do with you being abusive to others. It may have to do with setting boundaries.

Boundaries are about self-respect. Most people who are chronically abusive have low self-esteem or antisocial personality disorder, or they live in fear; they don't really love or respect themselves. If you allow someone to treat you poorly on a continuing basis, the mirror may very well be about loving and respecting yourself, and not a mirror of abusive behavior.

Of course, everyone can have a bad day, and sometimes we should try to mirror love and compassion to others. Trust me: there will be days that you need someone to mirror that back to you.

Sometimes you'll have an intense relationship with someone, perhaps a friend with whom you shared a similar crisis at the same time. For instance, in college you may have met someone you quickly befriended because both of your parents had recently divorced. You were each recovering from the emotional wounds of your family no longer being intact, despite the fact you always thought it would be. For a time you and your new friend did everything together. You were inseparable. But at some point, as the wounds healed, you both gradually moved in separate directions and maybe eventually lost contact with each other. This happens because the mirror of the emotional wound that brought you together ceased to exist and it was time for each of you to move on. By understanding the Law of Mirroring, we can positively apply it to all of our relationships, even those that are meant only to last for a short amount of time. All relationships are gifts that help us learn about ourselves and others.

The Law of Mirroring doesn't apply only to situations that require strenuous growth. When your soul is filled with love, joy, and happiness, it's those very traits that you can find in other people. Do you ever notice that most successful people seem to hang out with other successful people? Success is loosely defined as whatever success means to a given person. Artists tend to spend time with other artists, families with strong traditional family lifestyles tend to congregate in the suburbs, and business tycoons usually socialize with one another. This is the Law of Mirroring in action. Like attracts like. Even from the time we were in school we tended to hang out with people with whom we had common beliefs, ideas, and interests. If you played sports, were a cheerleader, or participated in the band, in all probability your closest friends did the same things you did.

If you don't like where your life is, look at those with whom you're spending time. Maybe they're mirroring your fears about making changes and moving forward. If you're trying to create something, find others who are doing it successfully. Watch what they're doing, and learn from it. Mirror their actions and ideas. Look for mentors—people who are doing what you want to be doing. For example, if you want to create a successful relationship with a man, don't spend *all* of your time listening to your recently divorced best friend complain that all men are incapable of having a healthy relationship. This isn't the mirror you want to emulate. Certainly, if you believe your friend's statement, then welcome the mirror and use it as an opportunity to grow and work through that belief.

When you're preparing to attract your ideal mate, think of the mirror you want reflected back to you. Become that person. Be kind, compassionate, supportive, and loving; take care of your physical health; develop new hobbies; and have a sense of humor if those are the things you're looking for in someone else. The wonderful thing about the Law of Mirroring is that you can create positive experiences by mirroring them to others.

The Law of Mirroring provides an opportunity for us to see aspects of ourselves reflected back to us. It reveals the truth, and truth can't be colored by justifications or excuses about why something exists. It merely points to what exists, and it's up to you to alter it or enhance that, depending on whether or not you like the reflection you see.

Elizabeth met Jay through an industry conference when she was dating a man whom she called the love of her life. She and Jay quickly became friends. Jay had been separated from his wife for two years. He was torn about whether he wanted to try to put his marriage back together or move forward.

Although Elizabeth knew she and her boyfriend were soulmates, the relationship was always a struggle and she never knew from day to day what the status of it would be. In some strange way she recognized that she and her friend Jay were each ironically mirroring the same issues—whether to stay or move on.

Elizabeth and Jay continued flirting at industry events and conferences for the next two years. Jay stayed separated from his wife but never got divorced, and Elizabeth stayed on the emotional roller coaster of her relationship with her boyfriend.

Finally, Elizabeth and her soulmate called it quits. She wasn't ready for anything serious, so at the next conference, when Jay flirted, she decided to take the bait. They began what she thought would be a brief fling, since they lived four hundred miles apart. The "fling" lasted on and off for the next three years.

At different points in the relationship Elizabeth would begin to get frustrated because Jay still was married, though he'd been living apart from his wife for seven years. And yet she wasn't sure she'd want to date him seriously even if he were available.

She struggled with the question "What am I mirroring in this relationship?"

Elizabeth's biggest complaint was that Jay was so indecisive. She considered herself a very decisive person. After all, she was the one who ended the four-year relationship with her soulmate.

Upon further reflection Elizabeth realized that she was mirroring indecision. After her heart had been broken she wasn't sure if she ever wanted to risk falling in love and being in a long-term relationship. She was also being indecisive about her career.

When Elizabeth became aware of her real issues, she decided she needed to make changes. Once she started taking steps to achieve her career goals and admitted to herself she wanted a long-term relationship, the energy between her and Jay changed. She realized that being in a three-year fling, even though it was long-distance, wasn't the energy she wanted to send the Universe about her ideal mate. She decided to end the sexual part of her relationship with Jay.

He, of course, began reaching out, but stayed indecisive about his marriage. Although Elizabeth wanted to remain friends, she knew this relationship couldn't be part of the future she wanted with her ideal mate.

Within six months of actually ending her relationship with Jay, she met a new man. She's not sure if he's the one for life, but she knows he's the one for right now.

Elizabeth learned that she had to be brutally honest about what the relationship was mirroring in her life. If she didn't want to keep that mirror in her life, she would have to change her beliefs and actions. Once she did, she was able to move beyond the mirror.

Kim is an office manager who lives in an upwardly mobile community in Dallas. One day she was meeting a male friend for a quick beer. As she was walking into the bar, a young man caught her eye, but she didn't pay too much attention because she quickly hooked up with her friend. They ordered a beer and started looking for a table. Out of nowhere, the young man who had caught her eye earlier said, "Would y'all like to sit with me?"

He, of course, didn't have a clue if the man with Kim was a date or just a friend. Since there wasn't anywhere else to sit, they joined him. He introduced himself as Jason and told them he was a singer and a graphic artist. Although Kim normally dated business types, she really enjoyed Jason's company, and there was an incredible physical chemistry between them.

At the end of the evening, Jason asked for Kim's phone number. She'd just ended a five-year relationship with a man she'd been engaged to and wasn't really looking for anything serious. She wanted to date and have fun.

The next day Jason called and asked Kim out for that Friday. The relationship quickly blossomed. The sexual chemistry between them was better than anything that Kim had experienced in her life. She enjoyed living in the moment and having fun with Jason.

While they were dating, Jason was focusing on his music career. He signed with a record label and spent time writing songs. Kim found this very interesting and began learning about the music industry so she could help him.

However, they did have their differences and problems. There was a four-year age difference—Kim was twenty-six and Jason was twenty-two—which brought about some maturity issues. Also, Jason wanted a more serious relationship than Kim was ready for. Within a couple of months the relationship fizzled.

Kim went on with her life and then, about two months later, Jason showed up at her doorstep. Kim was very reluctant to get involved again, feeling the relationship wouldn't go anywhere and they both might end up hurt. But the physical chemistry between them was very strong and she decided, "Life's too short; sometimes you just need to have some fun." The relationship was rekindled.

Jason was still focusing on his music, and Kim grew even more interested in the industry. They were at the music store one day, and Kim saw an ad for a band looking for a vocalist. She decided to call them and set up an audition.

When Kim and Jason got back together, it occurred to her that she wanted to help him with his career, but the relationship also had made her aware of the fact that she had an interest in performing and writing songs.

Although it was her first audition, the band liked her style and they all agreed to work together. They gave her their music and she wrote original lyrics. They are in the process of preparing to cut a CD and start playing in local clubs in Dallas.

Within a month of Kim's joining the band, she and Jason again broke up.

Kim believes Jason came into her life to help her realize she had an interest in creating and writing music. If she hadn't dated Jason at two different times, she might never have found music as an outlet to express herself. She's writing songs, singing, and having the time of her life. She's curious about who the next man in her life will be. She's eager to find out whether "he's the one" or just another teacher along the way.

_____

Your Emotional Suitcase

Each player must accept the cards life deals him or her. But once they are in hand,
he or she alone must decide how to play the cards.
VOLTAIRE

If I were packing a suitcase that included a swimsuit, suntan lotion, a beach ball, shorts, a sundress, and sandals, where would you think I was going? Probably, to the beach. What would you think if I told you I was going to Nome, Alaska, in January? You'd probably tell me I needed to pack warmer clothing. I'd have inappropriately packed to go where I was planning, but I would've been appropriately packed for somewhere that I had no intention of going.

Everyone carries what I call an emotional suitcase. Your emotional suitcase includes your past experiences, your fears and hopes. Some of the things in your suitcase give you healthy boundaries, while others take up space and may prevent you from packing what you need for your journey to your planned destination.

If you want to attract a lifelong mate, is your emotional suitcase filled with things that allow you to take that journey? Do you believe the relationship can happen? Or do you fear that it'll never happen? Do you think people are loving, considerate, and supportive? Or do you think they are out to use, control, and manipulate you?

What do you have packed in your emotional suitcase? Is it the right stuff for where you want to go? Are you carrying a small travel bag or a large trunk?

In "Law of Letting Go" (Part Four), I discuss in detail a technique Dr. Barbara DeAngelis uses to help you identify what's in your emotional suitcase. I encourage you to do the exercises to help you understand the emotional issues that you keep re-creating in your relationships.

Once you understand what's in your emotional suitcase, it's important to clean out the emotions that won't help you in your journey toward creating a lifelong relationship with your ideal mate. Clearing out old emotions that don't work for you may require you to forgive people in your past who have hurt you, either intentionally or unintentionally. You may have to forgive your parents, past lovers, or even yourself for making what you believe were poor choices. If you can't forgive, it's impossible to let go of past wounds that are taking up too much space in your emotional suitcase.

You also need to look at what's in your emotional suitcase that you want to keep there. Maybe you have good feelings about relationships because your parents, grandparents, or neighbors had one that you'd like to emulate. Focus on the things you want in your emotional suitcase. You may already have some of them in your suitcase, or you may need to start packing from scratch. Either way, you have a choice about what you want to carry with you. You just may need to take a little time and repack for the journey you now want to take.

Healing Old Emotional Wounds

We cannot become what we need to be by remaining what we are.
MAX DE PREE

There isn't one person walking on the planet who hasn't at some point in their life been emotionally hurt. Beginning in childhood, every person has experienced some degree of trauma. It may have been caused by parents, siblings, relatives, schoolmates, teachers, or complete strangers. The first time you felt hurt, abandoned, or not supported, it was a traumatic experience. It may have been when your mother left you at day care so she could work, or when your parents told you that you weren't good enough to pursue a dream, or when your classmates teased you. Without a doubt these experiences have continued in some form throughout your entire life. People either intentionally or unintentionally hurt us from time to time, just as we have hurt others. It's part of the human experience. However, it's your responsibility to decide how you respond to your emotional wounds.

"Woundology has become the new intimacy language," according to Dr. Caroline Myss, a medical intuitive who wrote *Anatomy of the Spirit.* She describes how, when we cling to our wounds, the negative energy affects our physical health and other areas of our lives.

We've moved to a point in our culture where we get most of our support and emotional reinforcement from others when we repeatedly describe how we've been hurt and damaged. Every time we lament over past wounds, it's like pulling the bandage off a cut that's just beginning to get a scab. It rips off the scab, and the healing process must begin again.

This probably affects women more than men. Think about when you meet a new girlfriend and the two of you begin to bond. How much of the bonding process is based on past experiences that you've had in common? How many of these experiences include coming from the same type of dysfunctional home, having had past boyfriends with the same negative behaviors, and sharing other experiences where you got to play the role of "poor me"? How much time do you spend talking and rehashing these same events over and over again, even though some of them may have happened many years ago?

Now, I'm not implying or saying that you shouldn't ever discuss your past wounds. It's a necessary part of the healing process, but if you keep reopening the wound for years after it happened, it'll never get healed. I know that sometimes it's hard to get the same attention and support from others if you focus on positive things that are happening in your life. But you have to remember that you attract into your life the things you focus on. If most of your focus is on past wounds and hurts, you'll find it impossible to create a life that doesn't re-create those wounds.

When you focus on your past hurts, it's difficult to give the new people you meet a chance to start a relationship with a clean slate. For example, you're on the phone with someone you just met that you like and want to get to know better, and they get another call. Thanks to the technology of call waiting, they ask to call you back, so you hang up. If your past wounds include an ex who had a habit of picking up other lovers and wasn't faithful (even though you thought you were in an exclusive relationship) and your ex used to ask to call you back and never did when another lover beeped through, you might naturally become fearful that this is a repeat experience. You might be thinking, "If they liked me, they would have asked to call the *other* person back." This would be a response to your past wound. But in all fairness, you would need to recognize and trust that this isn't your ex! You have to let someone have the opportunity to keep their word and call you back. When they return your call an hour later, you may find out that the call they took was long-distance from a family member or an old college buddy, or was from a colleague calling about a project at work. You just don't know the circumstances until you have had the opportunity to ask. You can't let your past wounds control your emotions: that's the first step to re-creating old relationships or self-sabotaging new ones. Would you want someone judging *you* based on wounds they received from past relationships? If not, then mirror what you would want in your new relationships.

Letting your wounds heal allows you to move into new situations and relationships with a clean slate. Yes, you're going to get new wounds, but the less you pull off the bandage to show them to other people, the quicker they'll heal. Once they're healed you can move closer to creating the relationship you want.

Sometimes it's necessary to seek professional help to heal old wounds. Many people don't like the idea of therapy, but if you had hundreds of cuts on your body and needed help disinfecting, stitching up, and bandaging the cuts, you wouldn't hesitate to go to the doctor. Emotional wounds still cause pain and can be just as damaging as cuts on your body. Just because you can't see them doesn't mean you don't need help. Unfortunately, it may be some of the very people you perceive as closest to you who are inflicting the wounds in the first place. A professional can help you objectively determine the original source of the wounds and how to begin the healing process.

Once you've learned how to treat your old emotional wounds, it's easier to heal new ones that you'll get. Although the pain of any wound will still hurt, you'll have an inner trust, faith, and knowledge that you'll recover from anything that happens to you.

Beliefs

If I have the belief that I can do it, I shall surely acquire the capacity to do it,
even if I may not have it at the beginning.
MAHATMA GANDHI

A friend of mine was complaining to me that she meets men she's
attracted to and is willing to begin a relationship, but ultimately it's either short-lived or never materializes. I asked what she thought was the
root of the problem. She replied that she didn't know but guessed she
was making poor choices. When you're preparing for a relationship it's
important to have faith and believe that you can find what you are looking for. If you *believe* that you always make poor choices, you'll attract
people to fit that role of "poor choice."

Beliefs are the imprints on your subconscious. They're the foundation for what you attract. They're the programming in your personal attraction magnet. If you believe that you can't find your ideal mate, then
that's the energy you put in your personal attraction magnet, and you'll
keep attracting people who aren't your ideal mate. If, on the other
hand—despite the fact that you've dated and had relationships with
what seems like hundreds of "this isn't the one"—you *believe* that you
just haven't met your ideal mate yet but they may be around the next
corner, then you might very well be right.

If *you* don't believe you can find the mate and relationship you want,
then why would the Universe send them to you? Of course, this means

you need to know exactly what you want in a mate and a relationship. Once you've decided what you want, then you must believe you can attain it. You can't have one moment when you think it's not possible. Doubt creates a lapse in the energy necessary to create what you want. It sends the message that you really don't *believe* you can have what you want or that you believe it doesn't exist.

I must remind you, you must believe you can have the relationship you want; however, it may not be with the person you've identified as your ideal mate. You can't *will* another person into being your ideal mate, despite your beliefs. I assure you, if the person you've decided is your ideal mate doesn't feel the same way about you, God has a reason for it and there's someone who's more compatible in your future. I know this is hard to accept if you really like or love someone, but you can't change someone else's free will. Free will is a gift God gave each of us. You wouldn't want someone that you didn't believe was your ideal mate, despite the fact that they believed you were ideal mates, to try to will you back into the relationship. You'd want them to respect your choice. Since you'd want someone else to respect your choice, you have to give others the same courtesy.

If you aren't attracting the relationships you want, examine your beliefs about relationships and members of the opposite sex. If you believe all men just want sex and aren't capable of sharing their emotions, or all women only want the things you can buy them, then that's probably what you'll attract. Make a list of your beliefs about relationships and men or women. Beside each item list experiences you've had that confirmed the belief. If you know what your beliefs are and understand where they originated, then you can begin to start changing them through affirmations, forgiveness, and new experiences.

Another way to gauge your beliefs is by your feelings. If you think you can create something but don't *feel* as if you can, then you probably don't believe you can have what you want. Feelings of doubt, fear, and wishful thinking can interfere in the flow of energy that allows you to believe you can create what you want. When you believe you can achieve something, then you are given a feeling of serenity and security and an inner knowing that it will happen despite any and all obstacles.

Remember when you were a child and you woke up on Christmas morning to find your living room full of the toys Santa left you? You believed that Rudolph led the sleigh of eight reindeer and Santa came down your chimney with a bag of the toys you'd wished for and left them at your house. You may even have heard the sound of deer hooves on your rooftop. As long as you believed in Santa Claus, he showed up at your house and left presents for you every Christmas. You never questioned if Santa would show up—you just knew and believed he would. However, when you were old enough to question how Santa made it to so many houses in one night and whether reindeer could really fly, a part of you was afraid to find out the answers because it might destroy the magic of Christmas. Asking too many questions and looking for too many facts could potentially destroy a belief. If the belief were destroyed, then Santa might not show up at your house. I still believe in Santa, and he still shows up at my house. The point is that a belief isn't about *logic*; it's about *expecting and believing in miracles.*

If you have a hard time believing you can attract the mate and the relationship you want, then start by believing in smaller things. Believe and trust that the next time you're at the mall there will be a parking space close to the store you want to go to. You really have to *believe* it. You can't have a moment's doubt. When doubt flashes through your mind, it cancels the belief. You may want to start believing you'll get a new job or piece of furniture, or take a trip. As you begin to manifest smaller, more tangible things in your life, it'll be easier to *believe* you can create anything, including the relationship you want with your ideal mate.

Part of manifesting your beliefs involves believing you *deserve to receive your request.* Sometimes we know what we want but think that we don't deserve it. Unless we believe we deserve gifts from the Universe, it'll be impossible for us to receive them. What do you believe you need to do to attract your mate? Do you need to change something in your life? Are you mirroring what you believe you want to attract? In order to attract your ideal mate, you must believe you deserve the relationship of your dreams. If you find you don't believe you deserve the relationship you want, look for the reason *why* you feel that way and begin to heal the wound. Always get professional help if you feel you can't identify the problem by yourself. Even though your friends may have the best of intentions, you and they may be mirroring similar issues, and therefore you can't get objective feedback. Often a counselor can provide the objectivity to help you see clearly the things that you want to keep or change and the best way to go about doing it.

Beliefs are the most powerful tool you have to create what you want. If, despite obstacles, you believe you can do or create something, you can. Keri Strug, Gloria Estefan, and Jimmy Carter are all people who believed they could come back after hardships and have made positive contributions to society. You can do anything you believe you can, even find your ideal mate. Remember, you're only looking for one person.

When Lisa was in college she had a serious boyfriend, but the relationship just didn't work out. During the next eight years Lisa dated and even had a couple of serious boyfriends, but she never met her ideal mate. They all seemed to be missing something that was essential to her.

Lisa is a devout Catholic. She believes in going to church every week, praying, and waiting until you're married to have a sexual relationship. She wanted to attract what she called a Ward Cleaver—a mate who was very loving, affectionate, religious, respectful, and responsible, and who understood her family values (she comes from a close family of ten kids) and would help her around the house.

When one of her relationships didn't work out, she sought counseling to help her change her attitude. She was twenty-eight and took this time to look at what she liked and didn't like about her life. Lisa realized that despite the fact she appeared confident, inside she was feeling bitter and negative. She began focusing on positive things, learning to listen to other people, and projecting herself differently. She became aware that life is about choices, and every choice has a consequence. You can either learn from your choices or repeat mistakes. She wanted to start making better choices.

Lisa came to the conclusion that she wasn't going to settle for anything less in a mate than what she wanted and believed she would find. Even if others thought her standards were too high, she had faith that if she hadn't met the man of her dreams, it hadn't been time for her to do so. She believes that if you're supposed to have a mate, God will guide you; but he won't bring him to your doorstep—you have to meet him halfway.

Lisa always went to church and prayed often, but she decided to become more involved in her church. She even helped organize a singles group. About one month after the singles group was formed, David joined it and started coming to the social activities.

Lisa knew she liked David and was attracted to him, but she considered him only a friend. That New Year's Eve the group had a party. David kissed Lisa at the stroke of midnight. By the end of January, they had started dating. They talked on the phone every night. Other men were still calling Lisa to ask her out, but she never accepted their dates. After dating David for a month, she realized that she wanted to see only him, but she didn't want to assume he felt the same way. Lisa recognized almost instantaneously that David had all of the qualities and values she was looking for in a mate. She decided to find out how David felt and asked him if he considered them an exclusive couple. He told her he did.

In April they broke up for two days. Lisa had made an incorrect assumption that David wanted to date another girl. When Lisa had asked if this was true, David had thought Lisa wanted to date someone else. The brief breakup reinforced Lisa's belief that you have to communicate exactly what you're really feeling.

By that May they were having "what if" discussions about the future, and in August David proposed. They were married the following June.

Lisa is now living her Leave It to Beaver life because she believes that she picked out a Ward Cleaver. She wasn't looking for a James Dean to change into Ward Cleaver. "Life is about having faith in God, being a good person, and making good choices," Lisa says.

Needs / Wants List

Every moment of your life is infinitely creative and the universe
is endlessly bountiful. Just put forth a clear enough request,
and your heart's desires must come to you.
SHAKTI GAWAIN

Part of preparing to find your ideal mate is deciding what you need
and want in a mate and a relationship. A *need* is something that you *can't
live without*; it's food, clothing, and shelter. A *want* is something that you
don't need to survive, such as caviar, Armani clothes, and a mansion in Palm
Beach. You *need* a home but *want* a mansion.

A relationship needs/wants list works in much the same way.

A *need* is something that you aren't willing to compromise about. It's
something that you find necessary regarding a relationship. It's not optional.

A *want* is something that you'd like, but it's negotiable. You may really want it, but if you don't get it, that's not going to ruin the relationship.

These lists will be different for everyone. There aren't any right or
wrong answers. It's important for you to understand what you need in a
relationship.

If you're asking someone else to give you something, then you need
to be willing to give back the same thing. It's the Law of Mirroring.

Make a list of traits you want in your ideal mate. Be brutally honest
with yourself. Be so specific that you think you're being silly. If you're a

man and really want a petite blond, brown-eyed ideal mate, then list it. You may realize that it's a want, and therefore negotiable instead of a nonnegotiable need, but list it. If you want someone who will participate a lot with the family, then you may not want to marry a workaholic, despite the fact that you find the money attractive. After you've made your list, determine whether each item is a *need* or a *want*.

Some of the things to consider when making your list:

- *Physical attributes.* Are you looking for someone who takes care of their physical body? Are you looking for someone who's healthy? Do you want a specific height? Do you like a certain body type? Do you find yourself attracted to a certain hair or eye color? Is there a chemistry that you find indescribable?

    When you meet someone, if you don't find them physically attractive, it's unlikely that you'll eventually find them romantically attractive. This can change if the situation wasn't conducive to romantic involvement when you initially met—for example, if you were each involved with other people and you suppressed your true feelings.

- *Emotional characteristics.* What do you look for in the way a person expresses themselves emotionally? Do you want someone who shares their feelings? Someone who wants you to solve their problems? Someone who's emotionally strong? Do you want someone who can nurture you? Do you like to be the nurturer? Do you want to share in the nurturing? How do you want them to express their anger, frustrations, and stresses? How do you want them to express their joys, successes, and feelings of love?

    The way your mate responds emotionally directly impacts the communication in your relationship, so be specific and determine your emotional needs and wants. For instance, if you need an announcement that your mate is going into their cave to work through a personal problem, then list it. Someone else might be fine if their mate didn't announce they were going into their cave. Some people may want hourly declarations of love, while others would find it suffocating. Think hard about your needs and wants and be honest.

- *Personality traits.* Are you looking for someone with a sense of humor? Do you want someone who wants to be the center of attention? Do you want someone who will let you be the center of attention? Are you looking for an introvert or extrovert? Do you want someone who spends time in deep thought? Are you looking for someone who is carefree and goes with the moment? Are you looking for a planner? Do you like making the plans? Do you want someone to discuss current events with? Are you looking for someone who will get your mind off current events?

  If you have to be the center of attention, then it might not work if your ideal mate needs to be the center of attention, too. You would end up competing for the spotlight. Be honest with yourself about what personality traits work best for you.

- *Financial habits.* Do you want someone who saves money? Someone who knows how to spend it? Someone who is financially responsible? Someone who is free-spirited with money? Do you believe in playing the stock market? Do you prefer savings accounts? Do you consider a home an investment? Do you believe in shopping with coupons or buying generic brands at the grocery store? Do you like designer clothes?

  Your attitude about spending money can potentially create the most grief in your relationship. It's important to know what you believe and what would be necessary to be compatible with your mate. If you want to have a healthy retirement fund and your mate wants to live for the moment, you'll have financial negotiating problems. Honesty is the first step to finding financial compatibility.

- *Spiritual beliefs.* Will your ideal mate believe in God? Will the two of you go to church or synagogue together? Do you believe that meditation is critical to communicating with God? Do you believe life is a spiritual experience?

Make sure that you know what spiritual aspects of your life are important to share with a mate. If you want to go to services with your mate every week and they don't believe in God, then you'll have serious problems. Spiritual beliefs are personal, but they can set the tone for a relationship.

- *Career objective.* Will your partner be ambitious? Will they be happy in their career? Will they put their family before their career? Will they put their career first? Do they have a job that requires them to travel? Will they have an understanding of your career priorities?

    You may think the fact that your spouse has a successful career is wonderful when you're dating, but if they spend eighty hours a week at their job and ignore your relationship, will it survive? Be honest about the role you want careers to play in a relationship.

- *Family.* Do you want children? Who'll be the primary caretaker? What do you believe is your responsibility to your childhood family? Will your mate run to mother every time she calls? Will your in-laws be spending long vacations with you? Do you want your mate to go home with you for every holiday? Do you want to ignore your childhood family?

    Never assume someone wants to be a parent. If one person wants children and the other doesn't, someone loses. Also, holidays eventually will arrive and you'll have to decide where you're going. Someone's parents will become ill and help will be needed. A sibling may need a loan. The point is, what role will your childhood families play in your life, and will you and your mate be in agreement about those roles?

- *Lifestyle.* Do you want to live in the city, or in a small town? Do you like to have lots of friends over? Do you hate company? Do you like to travel on a moment's notice? Do you like to have time to plan and pack? Do you want to attend the theater, or go to nightclubs, on Saturday night?

Some things about your lifestyle can easily be negotiated, but others will be more difficult. Know what you can and can't live with when you make your list.

- *Sexual compatibility.* How do you view sex? Is it a spiritual experience? An activity that's only entertaining? Are you a hopeless romantic? Do you like role-playing? Do you find costumes intriguing? Do you want lots of hugs and caresses? Do you want your partner to be verbally expressive?

  Sometimes chemistry isn't enough. You both need to find the same types of sexual activities appealing.

- *Values/morals.* Are you looking for someone who's honest, trustworthy, and fair? Do you want someone who values a relationship with a significant other? Do you want someone who believes in monogamy, or someone who believes in free love? Do you want someone who thinks it's OK to lie if it's in their best interest?

  If you're a police officer and your ideal mate thinks it's all right to deal drugs from your home, you may have different morals and values. Again, be honest about what you want in your mate.

- *Hobbies/fun activities.* Will you both enjoy playing golf? Going to the movies? Dancing? Partying? Being Little League coaches? Do you like entertaining friends and family? What will you do when you're together?

  This clearly should be an area that has several negotiable things, since you can't and shouldn't share everything with your ideal mate or eventually you'll each lose your individual identity and then struggle to find it. However, what *do* you want to share together? If your idea of fun is staying out till 4 A.M. and your mate wants to be asleep by midnight, can your relationship survive this?

This list isn't all-inclusive. If there is something that's really important to you that I haven't mentioned, then you need to add it. It may take you several days or weeks to complete this list. Look back on all of your past relationships and see what worked and didn't work. In fact, each relationship you experienced should have helped you determine your needs and wants. If you're still deciding what's on your list, then you may have more short-term mates to help you determine what works for you.

By being honest about what is and isn't negotiable for you in a relationship and mate, you're sending a clear request to the Universe. You'll even get to know yourself better in the process. Don't share your list with anyone who might not be supportive. Even if you think the items you've listed are silly, it's important to be specific. If you were building your dream home, you'd pay attention to every detail. You'd pick out everything, including the paint and wallpaper for each room, the handles on every cabinet and drawer, the types of lights, the bricks, the shrubs, and a million other small details. Why would you want to be any less specific when you're designing the blueprint for your ideal mate and relationship? Of course, you're free to change and update your list anytime you want.

Ellen had broken up with a live-in boyfriend of three years. She had reached a point where she wanted a commitment and the possibility of building a family; her boyfriend had no desire to make the kind of commitment she needed.

Within two months of breaking up, she accepted a date with John, a professor at the university where she worked. That summer, about eight months after they began dating, John went out to Wyoming to help out on the family farm. He flew Ellen out three times that summer and wanted her to come out again.

Ellen told John that she didn't like being away from the office for that much time.

John said, "What would it take to get you to come back out here?"

"I'm not coming back out. You can't just send me here and there when you feel like it," Ellen responded.

"What would it take?"

"I don't want anything," Ellen said. "I just wouldn't come under these circumstances."

"Would you do it under any circumstance?" John asked.

"I'd have to be committed to somebody. I can't keep traveling back and forth and jeopardizing my career," Ellen replied.

"What level of commitment would that have to be?"

"I'd have to be married," Ellen surprisingly said.

"Will you marry me?" John asked.

Ellen was shocked, but within six weeks they were married. Ellen moved to Wyoming, and she and John have been together for more than eleven years. Ellen learned that sometimes, when given the opportunity, you have to ask for what you want, even if what you want is news to you.

Intuition

Use your intelligence to support your intuition.
ANONYMOUS

While you're preparing yourself to attract your ideal mate, your intuition is the best compass to determine if you're on the right track. The more you learn how to become aware of and listen to your intuition, the more accurate you'll be in reading it and the easier it'll be to trust it. Unfortunately, your intuition isn't something that's tangible. It's a feeling you get in your body. Sometimes we call it a gut feeling, but in general it's a sensation that your whole body can feel.

If you aren't in the habit of listening to your intuition, start *now!* Intuition is something that can be developed with practice. Your intuition is always functioning, but in our logic-based world, intuition is often overruled. Let's think of a few times you probably feel your intuition. For instance, you're driving from your house to the neighborhood grocery store. For a brief moment you think you should take an alternate route, but then decide that's silly; you haven't a clue why you should go a different way than you normally would, so you don't. You reach the stop sign that you turn at, and you see there's an accident. Traffic is backed up, and you're stuck. Had you taken the alternate route you'd have gotten to the grocery store faster. Your intuition was guiding you, but you disregarded it in favor of logic.

Have you ever been thinking about a friend that you haven't spoken to for months or even years? Maybe you're even dreaming about them or another friend keeps mentioning the other person's name. Well, finally you pick up the phone to call the friend that you've been out of touch with and find out they're experiencing some type of personal crisis. You're glad you called, could lend an ear to listen, and maybe even help out. Your intuition was prompting you to reach out, and by trusting it, even though you didn't know why, you were able to be supportive to someone. You may have been their only bright spot that day.

As you become aware of small things that you're intuitively led to do, it'll be easier to follow your intuition when it comes to bigger things, like attracting your ideal mate. The challenge in listening to your intuition is to distinguish between what your *intuition* and what your *ego* is telling you.

You ego is fear based. That fear may be rooted in past experiences. For example, if you've dated people in the past who've lied to you and you're dating someone new, you may worry that they're lying to you. But the feeling is based on fear because of past experiences. It's accompanied by a chatterbox in your head pointing out all of the opportunities someone has to lie to you.

On the other hand, if your intuition were leading you to believe someone was lying to you, regardless of your past experiences you'd just *know* that someone wasn't being honest. When you're in moments that allow you to listen to your intuition, despite the fact that you may not like what you are feeling, that chronic chatterbox won't keep playing. When you intuitively know something, there's actually a divine *calmness* in your being.

When you're trying to get in touch with your intuition, it's important to let yourself be in a quiet, calm environment. It may be when you're meditating, sitting at the beach, or going for a walk in the park. But it's a time you can turn off your logical mind and allow yourself to simply *feel*.

If you're experiencing a lot of chaos and stress in your life, it's more difficult to stay in touch with your intuition. When your body isn't healthy, it's difficult to be centered. When you can't find even brief moments of inner peace so you can listen to your intuition, your ego will begin to take over. When your ego is the primary decision maker, logic is the foundation for the decisions you make. Logic is usually based on past experiences. For example, every time you touch a hot stove you get burned. Based on past experiences, logically you know that if you don't want to get burned, you shouldn't touch a hot stove. However, this same logic can't always apply to situations with people. Just because some people have always done something in the past that hurt you, you can't logically assume *other* people will do the same thing. Therefore, you must separate your logical thinking, which is attached to your ego, from your intuition, which is free of your ego's influence.

Sometimes your ego may want something so badly that you tell yourself that your intuition is signaling you to stay in a situation because everything will work out the way you *hope* it will.

For instance, you may feel you've met your soulmate. You're in love. However, the person isn't considerate of you, you know they lie about what they're doing when they're not with you, and they may ignore you except when they want you around for things that meet *their* needs. You try to relax and find your intuition. You feel it's telling you to stick it out and love will prevail. However, your chatterbox keeps playing, and you have to constantly justify to yourself why you are staying in the situation. Anytime you need to justify to yourself why you're staying in something that's hurting you, it's *not* your intuition telling you to stay. If, indeed, you're supposed to be practicing patience, tolerance, and unconditional love for another person and your intuition is leading you to this, once you've separated from your ego you'll find inner peace and serenity. You won't have to justify to yourself or others what you're doing. You won't feel a need to.

Ultimately, when you're listening to your intuition it's your phone line to God, or the universal forces. Unfortunately, it may not always be as clear as AT&T, MCI, or Sprint. With practice, you'll start noticing the small things. When you allow yourself to listen to and trust your intuition on a daily basis, then you'll be able to start applying it to the larger things in life with more confidence and ease. You'll then be able to trust it on emotionally risky ventures like relationships.

Angelic messengers often help us understand our intuition. They may be saying the very words that keep popping in your mind out of nowhere. Learn to respond to these ideas that seem to pop up out of the blue. If you do, your angels will keep helping you interpret your intuition.

As you become more aware of your intuition, you might find it leading you to certain stores, events, or parties that you might not ordinarily go to. It could be at these very places where you'll meet people who are critical to your personal growth, career, or significant relationship. If your intuition is telling you something isn't right about a relationship, then listen to it. Your intuition can help you avoid severe emotional pain if you learn to trust and follow it.

By recognizing and trusting your intuition you'll steer through life with as much ease as is humanly possible. It's your very own personal compass that can lead you to people, places, and things that are critical to your personal journey and the lessons you're here to learn.

Deion married Todd when she was twenty-two. At that time, she really didn't have any direction in her life; she was working at a grocery store and partying at night. Todd was leaving the air force and moving from Texas back to his hometown in Missouri. He had proposed during their short romance, but when they found out Deion was pregnant, that cemented the marriage proposal. Deion thought this was a chance to get a fresh start, but deep down she thinks they both knew it wouldn't be permanent.

After David was born, Deion gave away the baby bed, playpen, and car seat because she knew she would never have another baby with Todd. Deion decided she needed to start a career, so she went to nursing school at night so she could be at home with David during the day. She and Todd become more and more estranged.

Deion and Todd decided to take a trip and discussed trying to work things out. Deion wanted to save her marriage, but the first week back from the trip her husband didn't come home for three nights. At that point she found out he was seeing someone else. Within a month he walked out. She was dev-

astated that Todd didn't try to work out their problems as he'd said he would. What hurt even more was that Todd had lied about the fact he was seeing someone else.

During the next five years, Deion spent time in therapy working through childhood wounds. She learned to listen to friends while sorting through their advice and learned to take care of herself. She moved past the thought that she ruined her son's life and let go of the desire to get revenge on Todd. She learned to forgive, live in the present, and be grateful for the good things in her life. She learned that some days she was going to be depressed, but that tomorrow she might feel completely different. Each day represented an opportunity for a new beginning.

Deion dated, had a few relationships and even a couple of marriage proposals, but she knew none of these men were right for her. She believed that when she met the right man, God would let her know. She recognized that she didn't need a man to be complete. She also knew that you have to have inner peace if that's what you want in a relationship. You can't share something with someone if you don't have it.

She met Steve four years ago, when he coached her son's Pee Wee baseball team; his son was also on the team. They became friends through baseball and town events and when she got gas at the station where he worked.

Steve's marriage ended, and Deion found herself going by the gas station when she didn't have to. One day Steve said, "I went by your house one day."

"You did? Why didn't you stop?"

"I didn't want to interrupt one of your dates," Steve said.

"Oh, I haven't had any serious dates," Deion replied. "Just friends stopping by."

"Well, I may come over."

That weekend Steve, Deion, and David went to the movies. The next weekend Steve and Deion went on a real date. Deion had a feeling of "This is it." She wondered if she was crazy, but from that point on they were inseparable. Within three weeks Steve proposed. Deion knew it seemed too soon, but it also felt natural, and she put her faith in God.

When they started dating, Steve had asked Deion, "What do you want in your next marriage?"

"I want a friend," she said.

Deion knew that she and Steve were friends by the time they started dating. They were accepting of each other's children and wanted to create a loving, stable home. Within two months they were married.

"We're going through the challenges of merging two families, so it's not all roses without thorns, but it's nothing we can't work through," says Deion. "Despite what anyone thinks, you should always listen to and trust your own intuition."

Law of Attraction

You should always be aware that your head creates your world.
KEN KEYES JR.

Expand in consciousness—be ready to accept anything now, at any time.
EILEEN CADDY

In the section on the Law of Preparation we looked at things you can do to prepare your inner self for your relationship with your ideal mate. If you don't prepare your inner self for the loving relationship you want, it'll be impossible to attract it. So we worked on reprogramming your inner attraction magnet. Now, as we examine the Law of Attraction, we're going to work on things you can do to help bring your ideal mate into your life. These things are more tangible and ritualistic, and they help bridge the gap between physical reality and our subconscious mind.

We're going to look at how you can apply visualization, affirmations, meditation, hypnotherapy, goal boards, and prayers to help you attain your goal. If you've done your preparation work, these tools can help speed up the process of attaining your goals. Your preparation work is what allows you to become receptive to your ideal mate and anything else you want to create.

Again, these are only tools that can assist in the process. You can't circumvent experiences that you need to go through to assist with your soul growth, but you can stop repeating lessons once you've learned them. You'll move to new ones.

The tools described can help your dreams and goals feel more real and therefore bring them into reality. The more you practice using the attraction tools, the easier it will be to create what you want.

Lucy had recently moved from the East Coast to Phoenix, Arizona. She was finally settled and looking to meet her ideal mate. She'd been married two times and had had two long-term live-in relationships, but she wanted to find "the one." During the past year Lucy had worked hard to let go of ideas and beliefs that didn't serve her well. She spent time meditating and visualizing herself with her ideal mate.

Roger had also recently moved from the East Coast to Phoenix and wanted to meet his ideal mate. He'd been married five times, but he wasn't going to give up. He believed she was out there. He even placed an ad in one of the local New Age journals.

One day Lucy was at a psychic fair at a local New Age bookstore. As she was browsing through the books and walking down the aisle, she noticed Roger seemed to block her in. She thought maybe the Universe was sending her a message; she approached him, and they began a casual conversation.

Roger didn't appear to be Lucy's type, but she thought he was interesting. He told her he had placed an ad in the local New Age journal she was carrying. Once she got home she decided to read Roger's ad. It intrigued her, so she called him. They had a great conversation and decided to meet for coffee.

Lucy immediately recognized there was more to Roger than she'd originally thought. After they met for coffee the two became inseparable. They realized they were soulmates and within two months were living together.

The relationship had to struggle through a few communication issues, and each one had a few pieces of emotional baggage to clean out, but within a year they decided to get married. They have the same goals and beliefs, and each one shares in the desire for the relationship to grow and be nurtured.

Lucy thinks she and Roger are together because she listened to her intuition in the bookstore and started a conversation. She was even willing to take a risk and call him about his ad. "Sometimes God directs you, but you have to put forth the effort," says Lucy.

Visualization

If you can see yourself in possession of your goal, it's half yours.
TOM HOPKINS

Visualizing what you want to create is one of the most powerful tools you can use to actually help get what you want. Everything that you create is first recorded in your subconscious through your beliefs. However, your beliefs can become reality much quicker if you are able to visualize the outcome.

When they're trying to visualize, some people are worried if they can't get a clear mental picture of what they're trying to create. Some people *do* get crystal-clear pictures, and others may get more of a *feeling* of what they're trying to create. When you're visualizing your goals, if you don't get movie-perfect pictures, don't stop. Keep practicing. Eventually you may get the clear pictures you're looking for, but the important thing is to get a *feeling* about what you want to create. Feelings are your direct line to your beliefs and your intuition. The whole purpose of visualizing is to help you generate the feeling that you already have what you want.

In *Creative Visualization*, Shakti Gawain describes the four steps for creative visualization: set your goal, create a clear picture or idea, focus on it often, and give it positive energy. I'd like to discuss how to apply these steps.

Step one: *Set your goal.*
Your ultimate goal is to attract an ideal mate and create a loving relationship. But if you've had trouble in the past creating things you want, then you might want to start with something a bit smaller to help boost your confidence. Maybe you would like to pick up a new hobby, create a new job, or go on a trip. As you get better at believing and visualizing your goals, you'll be more successful at visualizing something you perceive as more difficult, like a relationship with an ideal mate.

Step two: *Create a clear picture or idea.*
In your mind visualize a clear picture of what you want to create. You need to picture this in the present tense—not future. Visualize it as if it's *happening now.* Let yourself feel it happening. You may want to create a goal board to help you make it more real (see the "Goal Board" chapter). Again, you may want to start visualizing a new job, a better relationship with your family, or taking a trip. Once you start *believing* in your power to create and manifest, it'll be easier to visualize your ideal mate.

Step three: *Focus on it often.*
Focus on what you want to create several times a day. The best time to do this is in the morning and at night, when your mind is the clearest and most receptive to suggestion. During the day you may want to look at your goal board or just take a couple of moments and think about what you want to create. Think of your goal in the present, as if it's actually happening.

Step four: *Give it positive energy.*
When you're meditating and visualizing your goal, see it in a white light. See yourself receiving the goal. Your feeling toward it needs to be welcoming, a feeling of acceptance—not anxiety, worry, or fear that you won't achieve your goal. Always think of it in a confident, loving way.

During the journey to finding your ideal mate, you'll be visualizing many things. You may be visualizing personal changes you want to make. Maybe you want to participate in a workout program, become more confident when you're meeting potential ideal mates, or reprogram the way you think an ideal relationship would function day to day. Once you meet someone who fits your needs list of ideal mate traits, you might want to visualize the two of you spending time together, having fun in a loving relationship. Don't forget you can't visualize a specific person into becoming your ideal mate, but if you're already in a relationship you can visualize how you would like it to go. You just can't be attached to a particular outcome.

"When you are attached to a particular outcome," according to Deepak Chopra, author of *The Seven Spiritual Laws of Success,* "it's based on fear and insecurity. Detachment is based on the unquestioning belief in the power of your true Self."

In relationships, detachment from the outcome is about allowing your higher self to act in your highest good.

Visualization allows you to see what you're trying to achieve; it therefore serves as a catalyst that allows you to feel as if you already have it. These feelings then funnel into your subconscious, which programs your beliefs. When you really believe you can create something, it's as close as your backyard.

Affirmations

Things do not change; we change.
HENRY DAVID THOREAU

Affirmations are statements we all make all of the time. They can either be positive or negative. More often than not we spend too much time affirming in the negative. Examples are "All of the good ones are taken," "I hate my job," and "I'm fat." Not one of those statements is solution-focused or stated in the positive. Your subconscious doesn't know the difference between positive and negative. It just knows what you tell it. If you're feeding your body an unhealthy diet and don't exercise, in most cases you'll gain weight, or at the very least begin to lose your skin's healthy glow. Your subconscious is the same way. If you feed it negative ideas, it'll start creating them in your life. On the other hand, if you feed yourself positive affirmations you can change your belief system and therefore what you create in your life.

Your positive affirmations should be based on your personal needs/wants list and any of your beliefs that may be limiting you from achieving the relationship you want with your ideal mate. To help boost your creation confidence, you may want to start by first affirming things that seem more achievable than attracting your ideal mate. Affirm the things you identified in "Law of Preparation" as changes you want to make.

Example affirmations are

I love myself.
I love the people who have caused pain in my life and release them.
My ideal mate is in my life now.
I forgive myself and others for creating wounds in my life.
Change is an opportunity for me to grow and explore.
I appreciate my body.
My ideal mate and I have a mutually fulfilling partnership.
Love is safe.

These are just a few examples. You should create affirmations that are specific to your needs. When you fill your subconscious with positive mental food, very soon your belief system will begin to agree with what you want to create. When your belief system is in agreement with your goals, you're one step closer to achieving those goals.

Silencing the Mind: Meditation

The miracle comes quietly into the mind that stops an instant and is still.
A COURSE IN MIRACLES

Unless you already listen to your intuition, it's unfortunately easy to not recognize it or just dismiss it when your mind is full of plans, regrets, and thoughts about your past or future. If you're not used to listening to your intuition, some form of meditation is the best way to still the mind. It allows you to get in touch with your intuition so you can recognize its feel.

Meditation is different for everyone. It's daydreaming, or staring at a pleasant scene, or clearing your mind. Some people can simply clear their mind, focus on their breathing—taking long deep breaths, releasing them slowly—close their eyes, and find that perfect Zen state. Others may choose to use chants or listen to calming music to help them get into a state of peace and tranquillity. Or you may need to focus more on breathing—learning to fill your body with oxygen, the true life force. If you have a difficult time moving into a meditative state, you may consider taking a class. Many classes are offered at local community centers, some churches, and even wellness programs.

You should think of meditating as you would brushing your teeth: something you automatically do every day for your spiritual health. You may even do it more than once a day, depending on what your energy diet has been that day.

If you haven't been meditating on a regular basis, you may want to start meditating for a small amount of time each day. Begin by meditating for five minutes before you go to bed. That will allow you to clear your mind before doing your visualizations and affirmations about your ideal mate. It's easier for your subconscious to accept new thoughts and ideas if you've cleared away the clutter from the day.

As you become more comfortable meditating, you might increase your meditation time in the evening and then add some in the morning or at lunch. Once you become accustomed to moving into a meditative state you'll find that you can achieve it on short notice and in almost any place. For example, you can meditate when you're flying, waiting in a reception office for an appointment, or just need a few moments to recharge your batteries.

Meditation is one of the oldest ways to connect with your higher self and to open the doors to your intuition. Your intuition is your direct line to God, or the universal force. By meditating on a daily basis you will allow yourself to find peace and serenity even in the most difficult times of your life. It'll also lead you to treasures, like your ideal mate.

Goal Board

What would you attempt to do if you knew you could not fail?
Dr. Robert Schuller

One of the ways to help attract your ideal mate is to create a goal board. This will help you actually see what you want. I recommend either drawing pictures of who you perceive is your ideal mate or cutting out a photo from a magazine of someone who resembles your ideal mate. Don't forget to include in your picture the things you would want in your life with this person. Do you want children, a particular type of home, specific vacation destinations, a twenty-fifth-anniversary party, and lots of open affection between you? Put it on your goal board. You may want to get a big poster board for this. View it as a mural of the life you want to create. You may add to it as you decide new things you want to include. Put it in a place that you can see often. Don't hide it. That may send a hidden message to the universe that it's not a priority. You may want to put it in your bedroom. Make sure it's where you can see and focus on it daily.

I frequently spend time in Japan and have the opportunity to help people there. During a recent trip, I got to help several people work on attracting their ideal mates. My goal is to live there part-time in the very near future.

Goal boards are one of my favorite ways to help people visualize exactly what they want to create. It gives them a tangible picture. On several occasions I recommended this technique to the people I was helping. I suggested they cut out of magazines photographs that resembled what they envisioned as their ideal mate. I also recommended that they cut out pictures of what they wanted the relationship to include.

During my stay, two different people whom I'd seen during my first week in Japan came back to tell me that they had done a goal board and manifested their ideal mate. In fact, one gentleman said the woman he attracted was almost a twin to the woman in the picture he put on his goal board.

Goal boards help your subconscious get a clear picture of what you're trying to create. This of course plays into the belief system that programs your personal attraction magnet.

Hypnotherapy

The road to success is always under construction.
ANONYMOUS

A licensed hypnotherapist can help you deal with, heal, and get beyond old wounds that may be blocking you from being able to create the new beliefs that will help you attract your ideal mate. Hypnotherapy allows you to process emotional pain as a third party, therefore allowing detachment. When you're processing emotional pain as a third party, you're watching the scene as you would a movie. You're one of the actors in the scene. Once you've processed the emotional pain, you'll begin to heal. As you heal you'll be able to put new ideas and thoughts into your subconscious that allow a new belief system to form. You can also receive positive thoughts and affirmations when you're in a hypnotized state. Suggestions you receive when you are hypnotized go directly to your subconscious. Remember, hypnotherapy should be done only by a reputable professional whom you trust.

Where's My Guardian Angel?

If you are seeking creative ideas, go out walking.
Angels whisper to a man when he goes for a walk.
RAYMOND INMON

I believe guardian angels are with us at all times. In my book *Your Guardian Angels,* I go into great detail about their history, what they do, and how you can communicate with them. Your guardian angels can help prompt your intuition and direct you to do things you might not otherwise think of.

Ask for their assistance in attracting your ideal mate. But if you ask for their assistance, listen for their response. Don't ignore those thoughts that just seem to pop into your mind out of nowhere and for no reason at all. Those thoughts may be your angels talking!

In many cases your guardian angels can help you find something you might not have found without their assistance, or prevent you from making a mistake in a current relationship. You just have to ask, and then be aware of their presence. The more you listen to them, the more you'll hear them.

Shelia had recently become involved with a neighbor, Scott, whom she'd known and been friends with for about five months. Neither Shelia nor Scott was willing to come out and ask questions about what the other person wanted, so the relationship was on an insecure foundation.

One week when Scott was out of town, Shelia accepted a UPS package for him. He was going to pick it up at some point.

Scott returned from his trip Saturday night, but he didn't pick up his package. On Sunday, Shelia called to see if Scott wanted to watch a movie that night. He replied, "Sure, I'll call you later."

That afternoon, Shelia could see Scott's car wasn't home, yet he hadn't called to confirm the movie. By 7:30 P.M. Shelia was getting angry because Scott wasn't home and still hadn't called. She felt she was being stood up.

She decided to take a drive and go look at the Christmas lights, but before she left she took his package and dropped it off at his apartment without a note. She got into her car and started driving. For no reason she began feeling extremely sleepy. Although she was disappointed and wanted to do something fun to take her mind off it, she decided she should go back home and maybe go to bed early.

Scott still wasn't home when she returned, but she was too tired to care. When she went into her apartment, for some reason she picked up her office phone and realized she had a message on it. She listened to it and it was Scott calling to tell her he was on his way home from the mall and did she still want to watch a movie? She immediately ran to get the package from his doorstep before he arrived home.

Although there was clearly some miscommunication between them, Shelia believes it was her guardian angels that made her feel too sleepy to drive around and prompted her to pick up her work phone. Otherwise Scott would have gotten home, found the package left in front of his door without a note, and assumed she was mad. This would only have added to the insecure foundation of the relationship.

That was two months ago, and since then they've even had a "state of the relationship" discussion. They aren't looking too far down the road, but it seems the relationship is right for them now. Shelia believes her guardian angels are assisting her with the lessons in this relationship.

Prayer

Prayer: what you do when nothing else seems to work.
ANONYMOUS

Never underestimate the power of prayer. If you believe in any God or a universal power, then ask for assistance in creating your ideal mate. If you participate in a religious or spiritual group that does prayer circles, ask to be put on the list. You can never have too many people asking for help on your behalf.

When your prayers are answered, make sure you recognize that and respond with gratitude. It's fine to keep repeating your prayer, but remember: if God hasn't answered it, there may be a good reason. Unanswered prayers may just mean the timing isn't right. You have to have faith and trust that all things happen when they are supposed to and that God does know best.

Lights, Camera, Living

Eighty percent of success is just showing up.
WOODY ALLEN

We've been talking about how you can do inner work and make changes in your life to help you prepare for and attract your ideal mate. However, you can make all of the changes in the world, but if you're not willing to do things differently, it'll be hard to find your ideal mate. By doing things differently I mean *changing your normal routine.* If you usually go home as soon as you get off work, order takeout, and rarely venture out beyond your local grocery store, then unless your ideal mate delivers takeout, is standing in line behind you at the checkout counter, or is a neighbor, it may be hard to meet them. On the other hand, if you spend every night at your local bar and you get frustrated that you keep meeting people who may have drinking problems, aren't looking for a relationship, and have seemingly shallow lives, you might want to consider getting involved in other activities.

As we discussed in Part One, "Law of Love," it's important for you to have a full, balanced life for many reasons: you'll be a whole, complete person whom someone would want to date; you'll live in the land of the living and not in the land of waiting and hoping that your ideal mate will just show up at your office or front door.

Sometimes, even if you don't want to, it's important to get out and socialize. You need to put yourself in places where you can meet new people. I'm reminded of the interview Barbara Walters did with Barbra Streisand and James Brolin on 20/20. They were being introduced by friends who'd invited each of them to a dinner party with several other people. They both said that they almost canceled, but didn't. Maybe they were listening to their intuition or guardian angels. Once they met, they quickly knew they were meant to be together. My point is that even though you may not want to go somewhere, you never know whom you might meet.

I'm not suggesting that you become a partyer if that's not your personality; just make a point to do things you enjoy with other people or alone. If you enjoy going to church, theater, or bookstores, or volunteering to help others, then do it—anything that gets you out and living life.

Dan was a twenty-eight-year-old college student who'd recently broken up with his girlfriend. Although the relationship was serious, he'd realized that it wouldn't last. So, to help mend his broken heart, he toured Europe with his whole family—both parents, stepparents, grandmother, brothers, sisters, and even some cousins.

He met Renee in the lobby of a hotel in London. She was a friend of his cousin's and part of the tour. Throughout the rest of the trip Dan and Renee talked a lot, but their relationship didn't blossom into a romance.

Toward the end of the trip Dan's cousin went to Renee and said, "Dan kind of likes you," and Dan's brother-in-law came up to him and said, "Renee kind of likes you." Actually, neither of them had ever said any such thing.

This disinformation pushed their friendship in the direction of romance. After the trip, Dan returned to California and Renee went back to Kentucky. Dan decided to send her flowers. Renee called to thank Dan, and he ended up inviting her to California.

At this point they both thought the romance would be short-lived because of the distance. But during the next year, they started visiting each other about once a month, writing, and talking on the phone.

One weekend they met in Nashville. Dan told Renee, "If you get a tattoo, I'll move to Nashville." That night Renee got a rose and Dan got a shark tattoo.

After graduating college, Dan moved to Kentucky for about six months before finding a job in Nashville. Those first six months were a combination of the honeymoon phase of the relationship, adjusting to living together, and the stress of Dan looking for a job. When they were struggling, Dan thought for a day or two, "Oh, God, I made a mistake." But things always worked out.

Shortly after Dan moved to Nashville for his job, Renee joined him there. A year later, they were married. Two years later, they had their first baby. They've been together for six years.

Dan credits the year they were living in separate states for preparing them to be together. He said, "You learn a lot about what a person likes and doesn't, and what they think, when you're forced to verbally communicate and can't spend a lot of time together because of distance."

Practicing Silence

It is important from time to time to slow down, to go away
by yourself and simply BE.
EILEEN CADDY

We live in a time when we have a tendency to announce our every thought, action, and intention simply because we can. People share their most intimate secrets on television and radio shows. However, I'm going to tell you that if you really want to attract something in your life, then it is *not* in your best interest to share that goal with everyone. Think of your goal as a cake. Every time you share what you're trying to create, you give away some of the cake. If you aren't careful, you'll give away the whole cake.

When you share, most people will either give you advice or make a judgment about your goal. Either way, you pick up negative energy through their judgment or doubt because of their advice. This contradicts the positive energy, affirmations, and visualizations that you're applying toward your goal.

I'm not saying you can't share with anyone. But be selective about who it is. Make sure that person will listen and offer advice only when asked. It needs to be someone who won't judge or criticize the goals you've set for yourself, but instead be supportive.

Also, if you're ever in a relationship that's abusive, you need to tell someone and leave it. Practicing silence isn't about keeping secrets to protect someone while other people are getting hurt, including yourself.

When you meet someone who might be a potential mate, don't share details about the relationship right away. Undoubtedly your family and friends, even those with the best of intentions, will make judgments about the progress of the relationship. It's *your* relationship, and if you and the person you're involved with are content, then that's all that counts. As one of my friends says, "You don't have to call a board meeting of your friends to have a relationship."

Practicing silence gives you an opportunity to learn to trust your judgment and intuition and develop your own personal relationship with God.

Risk

Sometimes the only way for me to find out what it is I want to do is go ahead and do something. Then the moment I start to act, my feelings become clear.
HUGH PRATHER

To be happy one must risk unhappiness.
JUDD MARMOR

The only way you can actually begin a relationship with your ideal mate is to be willing to take normal emotional risks involved in having a relationship. You have to be willing to get hurt. It's never a goal to get hurt, and in order to prevent getting hurt you may have built walls to protect you. These very walls may be keeping out the very people you want to attract.

Apply the Law of Mirroring: would you want to attract someone who's so afraid of getting hurt that they let the fear control their relationships with other people? If this isn't what you want to mirror, you have to be willing to let *your* walls down enough to let someone in.

I'm not suggesting that you take unnecessary risks that you aren't comfortable with. For instance, if you like someone and you don't have any reason to believe they like you in return, then you may not want to announce your feelings to that person. Of course, if you're a risk taker you may want to throw caution to the wind and see what response you get back. Remember, you have to respect each person's right to free will, their choices about you and your relationship or potential one. By taking a risk, though, you may get the very response you want.

You should always applaud yourself when you go out on a limb. Even if you fall and get hurt, you'll recover. The alternative to taking risks isn't any less painful; it's just a different kind of pain. It's one of loneliness and fear. In *Grumpy Old Men*, Ann Margret's character says, "The only regrets you have are the risks you didn't take."

Darlene believes romance can come when you least expect it. She had read about Leo in the local Fort Lauderdale newspaper because he had completed a solo circumnavigation around the world in his boat and had just arrived in Fort Lauderdale.

Darlene, who was sixty-one, decided to write Leo (who was still in Fort Lauderdale) a letter of admiration, because he was sixty-six and following his dream. She included a picture of herself and her twin sister and said if he'd like to get together for coffee, please call. She was eager to talk to him about his adventures and how he'd achieved his goal.

Leo received hundreds of letters, but he picked hers out and gave her a call. Her twin sister wasn't home, so Darlene met Leo alone on his boat for coffee the day he called. They chatted, and it was as if they'd known each other for a long time. It felt very comfortable.

A couple of days later, they went on a first date, to see Sleepless in Seattle. *A few days later they went dancing, and both knew this was very special. "I hadn't really been looking for romance, so it was a pleasant, unexpected surprise," said Darlene.*

Earlier Darlene had made a wish list about the traits she wanted in an ideal mate. It included someone who was loving, kind, compatible, good-natured, of spiritual like mind, financially comfortable, and in good health, and who accepted her family and enjoyed movies, theater, dancing, cooking, and travel. Cooking was especially important since Darlene doesn't like to cook. When she made this list, it was more for fun than anything serious. But it did send a message to her subconscious.

Oddly enough, many months before she met Leo, out of the blue a store checkout clerk announced, for no apparent reason, "You'll meet someone in July or August, and you'll be happier than you've ever been."

Darlene met Leo in July. That Christmas he proposed to her in her Christmas card. They were married the following March. They sailed across the Atlantic for their honeymoon. They've been together for five years, and it's better than anything Darlene ever dreamed it could be.

Detachment

To see a miracle, let go of expectation.
ANONYMOUS

For every statement that I've made about preparing, planning, and taking steps to attain your goal of finding your ideal mate, I will now tell you to *detach from the final outcome.* I know it's an unfair dichotomy. I'm saying, "Want something, put effort into getting it—and then detach from the outcome."

But when you're attached to the outcome, it's like mixing the ingredients of a cake, pouring them into the pan, and then insisting on holding the oven door open and trying to watch them bake. If you don't shut the oven door, all the heat escapes and your cake can't cook at a constant temperature. Creating what you want is very similar. If you are always monitoring the progress of your goal, it can't form the way it's supposed to.

Also, as good as you can imagine a person, relationship, or anything else you want, God can imagine it *better.* You don't want to miss out on the first-class gift that God can bring into your life just because you're willing to settle for a coach ticket. When you hear about people who've achieved something they've dreamed of, you often hear them say the experience is better than they could've ever imagined. My point is that when you're not attached to the outcome, there's room for it to become what it's supposed to be, not just what you *think* it should be.

"In detachment lies the wisdom of uncertainty. . . . in the wisdom of uncertainty lies the freedom from our past, from the known, which is the prison of past conditioning," says Deepak Chopra in *The Seven Spiritual Laws of Success.* "And in our willingness to step into the unknown, the field of all possibilities, we surrender ourselves to the creative mind that orchestrates the dance of the universe."

Although I'm psychic, my story about finding my ideal mate is just like yours. Even though I've found my ideal mate, I too have had previous relationships in which I thought I'd found him, only to realize each one was just another teacher along the way. It would sometimes seem to me that because I was always helping other people find their mate through my psychic abilities and spiritual counseling, I was always being tested on the advice I gave. The saying "We teach best what we most need to learn" seemed to be a lesson for me.

My point is that I know and understand the loneliness and frustration of wanting to find your ideal mate and not being able to. I began programming myself many years ago to meet my ideal mate. I practiced the Law of Love, by learning how to love myself, leading a full, balanced life, following my intuition, and living in a state of love.

I would attract mates that were ideal for a time, to help me learn lessons that my soul needed, and I'd eventually have to practice the Law of Letting Go. I learned to never hold anger or negative feelings toward anyone and to visualize them in white loving light. My faith and trust in God and the natural order of the Universe allowed me to believe that if someone wasn't supposed to be in my life, it was best for each of us to move forward.

Finally, I believed that you have to put the actions described here, in "Law of Preparation and Attraction," into place. I actively wrote out my needs/wants list, created a goal board, meditated daily, prayed, asked for angelic assistance, stated daily affirmations, visualized meeting my mate, worked with a hypnotherapist (in fact, the very week before I met Jim, I'd been hypnotized and told my subconscious that my ideal mate would arrive in divine order), and lived life so I could create opportunities to meet my mate. I also recognized the need to detach from my request and trust that God would lead me to my ideal mate. The very qualities and traits that I put on my needs/wants list, I worked on in myself. For example, I appreciate physical health, so I take care of myself by exercising and eating healthy.

While I was doing these things to prepare to meet my ideal mate, Jim was also preparing to meet his ideal mate. Jim had been taking a serious look at his life and deciding what did and didn't work. He realized he really wanted to be with a life partner. He'd started letting go of old beliefs that he didn't like. One day he was at a water fountain and threw in his coins to make a wish. He wished for "the woman of my dreams." At that moment he sent his request to the Universe and let it go.

Jim's brother had just started a business in Fort Lauderdale and called Jim to see if he could come down and help him. Jim, who's a chef by trade, thought going to help his brother would be the right thing to do. Jim's brother had started a window-washing business for area hotels. Jim happened to be working with his brother at the hotel in which I was staying.

The night before I met Jim, I had been looking out my balcony window. I noticed ropes hanging and thought someone would be cleaning the windows the next day. The next morning I had gotten dressed to begin my day's activities, but minutes before I was about to leave, I opened my curtains and looked out the balcony window. Jim was literally coming out of the sky on a scaffold when our eyes met.

We were instantly attracted to each other. I saw an opportunity and took advantage of it. I opened the window, gave him my card, and offered him a free psychic reading.

Jim's brother told him, "I think she likes you," but Jim didn't believe it.

Since he was shy, he had his brother's fiancée call and set up the appointment for the psychic reading. After setting up the appointment, she told Jim, "I think Linda was disappointed you didn't call yourself."

Later that night when we got together, we recognized we'd been looking for each other forever. We instantly bonded at the physical, mental, spiritual, and emotional levels. Our holistic relationship began.

We were prepared to take advantage of it and be grateful for the opportunity to share our lives.

We mirror all of the positive traits we each wanted to attract in a mate. We were willing to take a chance, and it paid off.

We've become partners in love, work, and life. Thanks to my faith and belief in God and my faith that everything happens when and as it should, meeting Jim has made my dreams a reality.

If you take a trip to your local bookstore you'll find more books than you can count about how to get married, find a mate, and have a relationship. Some of the books do offer good advice and tips. However, many just tell you how to play games with the opposite sex. If you wouldn't want someone treating *you* the way the books describe, I suggest you don't read them, and certainly don't apply to someone else the techniques described. If you're looking to get married to someone who plays games and isn't capable of having a lifelong relationship, then those are the books for you! They'll teach you how to mirror and attract people who respond to tactics and not real love.

It's true, men and women are different. We respond differently to relationships and situations, but we all have in common the need to be loved unconditionally. When you're clear about what you want to attract in an ideal mate and you make the commitment to become like the person you want to be with, you can attract your other half. I'm not saying it's easy or will happen overnight. In fact, it may very well happen when you least expect it because you've actually detached from the outcome. But you'll have done your inner work to prepare yourself for the opportunity. Destiny or luck is when opportunity meets preparation.

At any moment destiny may come knocking at your door. By following the techniques described in "Law of Love" and "Law of Preparation and Attraction," you'll be living a balanced life that is full of love and actively preparing yourself for the opportunity to meet your lifelong mate.

Until one is committed, there is hesitancy, the chance to draw back, always ineffective-ness. Concerning all acts of initiative (and creation), there is one elementary truth, the ignorance of which kills countless ideas and splendid plans: that the moment one defi-nitely commits oneself, then Providence moves too.

All sorts of things occur to help one that would never otherwise have occurred. A whole stream of events issues from the decisions, raising in one's favor all manner of unforeseen incidents and meetings and material assistance, which no man could have dreamed would have come his way.

SCOTTISH HIMALAYAN EXPEDITION

Do all the good you can, in all of the ways you can, to all the souls you can in every place you can, at all the times you can, with all the zeal you can, as long as ever you can.

JOHN WESLEY

Part Three

❧

Law of Maintenance

We are what we repeatedly do. Excellence, then, is not an act, but a habit.

ARISTOTLE

$\mathcal{M}$ost people know more about the maintenance requirements of their cars than of their relationships. One reason is that unlike relationships, cars come with a maintenance manual. Unfortunately, in relationships it's usually a little more difficult to diagnose the exact maintenance requirements, and relationships *do* require routine maintenance.

A problem with your car is usually obvious: the air conditioner makes a sound, your tires show wear, or you look at your odometer and realize your oil needs to be changed. Your car requires that you do routine maintenance like putting in gas, washing it, and changing the oil and filter on a fairly regular basis. Then you'll have to do a tune-up, check the brakes, and monitor your tire tread. At some point you'll probably have to replace the battery, get a new air conditioner, and change your belts, hoses, and other equipment as it wears out.

Relationships are the same. On a fairly routine basis you have to communicate your needs, create romantic moments, and feel loved. Occasionally, you'll have to evaluate and set your short- and long-term goals and determine if everything is working for each of you. You may even need to put your relationship in a "therapist shop" to help you understand and replace old thought patterns so you can continue your relationship in a healthy way. My point is that even under the best of circumstances, like when you've attracted your ideal mate, you'll still have to work to maintain the relationship in peak condition.

You probably think of your ideal mate as your soulmate. A soulmate is your other half, that special person who can give you a sense of completion. When you're in their presence you feel a loving energy that's stronger than anything you could ever imagine. Of course—to apply the laws of physics—for every positive there's also a negative. The negative to being in the presence of that much love is the *fear that you'll lose it*. So your ideal mate, or soulmate, will be the gateway to emotional highs that you've never experienced, and they'll also magnify your fears beyond your worst nightmares.

I share this not to alarm you, but so you'll realize that although you thought finding your ideal mate was the toughest part of having the relationship that you've always wanted, the opposite is true. Once you find your soulmate, the real work is *just beginning*. However, the real work can bring out the best in you and your mate. This relationship is the one that allows you to work through the fears that have kept you from being everything you've wanted to be and living your dreams. But if you ignore routine relationship-maintenance needs, you'll spend all your time and efforts attempting to predict and repair what's broken or is about to break in your relationship.

Each person who comes to the relationship is somewhat like a used car. Don't take this wrong, but a used car requires more routine maintenance than a brand-new car right off the dealer's lot. We all have a certain number of miles on us that began the moment we were born. Our first ideas about significant relationships began with the one we saw the most: the one between our parents. As we got older we'd compare that one with the relationships of grandparents, aunts, uncles, neighbors, and the parents of our friends. You even picked up ideas about how you thought a relationship should be from watching TV and movies and listening to songs. When you had your first crush and you met your first boyfriend or girlfriend when you were either in preschool or in elementary school, you may have even planned your wedding! Did you ever play house during recess? The little boy might have gone off to work, and the little girl stayed home to take care of the dolls, clean house, and cook dinner, if you were emulating *The Brady Bunch* or *Leave It to Beaver*. Realistically speaking, most homes are more likely to be a mirror of *Rosanne, Step by Step,* or even *The Simpsons*—a little dysfunctional, perhaps a blending of more than one family, and somewhat unorthodox. But even as children, we liked to mirror our ideal of perfection.

As you got older you began thinking your romances should be more like the ones you see on your favorite day- and nighttime soap operas or read about in romance novels. Of course, most of these characters involved in steamy romances never seem to have to deal with life's realities, such as paying the bills, taking care of children or parents, or even doing their own shopping. The images of romantic relationships and life that you see portrayed on the screen are rarely anything resembling reality. But these images *do* influence our subconscious thinking unless we're actively replacing them with healthy, realistic ones.

Ironically, relationships in *real* life can be better than the ones you see on TV or at the movies. Why? Scripts rarely let a relationship build over time, so the relationships do not have a solid foundation or naturally evolve into something mutually fulfilling and loving. Screen relationships are based on passionate moments designed to stir an emotion in the viewer, but they're rarely based on love. In real life you can have many passionate moments based on the love necessary to carry you through the less than passionate moments that all relationships must experience.

Once you've met your prospective ideal mate, you'll begin a journey together to find out if you're indeed a compatible match for long-term commitment. But this is a journey and *not* one-stop shopping. Anytime you merge the free wills of two individuals, no one can predict if both of those people will be willing to stay on the same path of the journey.

When you're on any journey, it's important to know *exactly* where you are in the journey, even if it's recognizing that you're *lost*. If you're planning a trip and you'll be gone for more than a day, then you'll have to pack before you leave. If you're flying before you leave, you'll have to get a ticket and make arrangements to get to the airport. If you're driving, you may need to fill up your gas tank before you leave. Once your trip begins, you'll be at different points throughout the journey. You may have to stop to eat lunch, refill your gas tank, or have time to check in your luggage at the airport. Then once you've arrived at your destination, you'll still have different things to do, depending on the circumstances of the trip. The point is, when you're taking a trip you have to be focusing on *the task in front of you,* not spending your time and energy thinking about the destination or you'll never get there. Relationships are the same way.

A friend of mine was visiting Sedona, Arizona, and someone at a restaurant gave him a hand-drawn map to what they called "the most sacred Indian site." He decided to drive to it in his rental car the next morning. The dirt roads were narrow and winding. A jeep would've been a better choice of transportation. After about fifteen miles, he came to a sign stating the roads would become even more steep and winding. Thinking he was only a couple of miles from the site, he decided to leave behind his rental car and walk. Since he thought he would be hiking for only a couple of miles, he didn't take any hiking supplies, like water, food, or a first-aid kit with him. After four miles of hiking on a winding, hilly, desolate dirt road, he found the site and hiked around for a while.

Walking back to his car, he realized how remote the site was. He hadn't seen another car or person in hours. He could hear the wildlife on both sides of the dirt road. He kept going up and down hills hoping to see his car after each one. He kept looking in the distance for it. He was getting hotter, more thirsty, and tired. It'd been hours since he'd had any water. Finally, he tripped on a rock in the road and fell down. He realized at that moment that he'd better start looking at what was in front of him and quit looking too far ahead, or he might fall and really get hurt. In the immediate moment it was more important for him to watch the steps in front of him than to gaze in the distance looking for his car. Eventually he'd find it. But if he fell and ended up with a sprained ankle, it would definitely slow down his journey.

Sometimes we get so focused on what we know or think we're heading toward that we trip while taking the steps in front of us, which we must take to actually get us to the destination. Tripping either slows us down or completely stops us because we get emotionally hurt and have to heal. We'll all trip from time to time, and it doesn't mean that we can't recover, but we'll trip less if we're looking at the steps in front of us instead of the ones down the road.

In new relationships it's important to realize exactly where the relationship is so we'll know which steps are in front of us and can take those without tripping (at least not too much) so we'll reach our destination faster and in good shape.

Stages of a Relationship

Great things are not done by impulse but by a series
of small things brought together.
VINCENT VAN GOGH

Once we've met someone we feel is a kindred spirit, it's often easy to just jump from "Hey, we just met and I'd like to get to know you better" to "Hey, we're soulmates and we're going to spend the rest of our lives together." When both partners have done their inner preparation work, these types of relationships can happen. But more often than not, when we meet our ideal mates, we're still working through some of our emotional baggage. Although we may *think* and *believe* a specific person is our ideal mate, we're still creatures of habit and need time to make sure and to adjust to the idea of sharing our life.

A significant relationship occurs when two people agree to come together and share their lives. Both partners are participating in the physical, spiritual, emotional, and mental growth that makes the relationship holistic. However, you won't get to this point overnight. It's true that some people meet and instantly begin a life together that works. But more often than not, you'll go through a few moments that resemble riding a roller coaster. Even in the best of relationships there will be ups and downs, even if both of you have done your individual preparation work.

Those roller-coaster moments are there to teach lessons to each of you. The lessons may be about letting go of fear, unconditional love, living in the moment, joy, happiness, or experiencing bliss. We attract what we're focusing on and believe, because our experiences are a reflection of our *true* beliefs. Despite our best efforts to live in love, we're all human and will, on occasion, have to cope with our fear-based beliefs. Just be prepared and keep focusing on the love in your relationship so you can generate more of it.

Remember, even though you may have met your ideal mate, your relationship will still have to go through certain stages. By understanding these stages, it's easier to know what to expect as the relationship progresses. Your expectations of a friend you met yesterday are vastly different from those of someone who's been your best friend since grade school. Yet when we meet the person who we believe is our ideal mate, we often have expectations of them and the relationship that may not be realistic for that stage of the relationship. Maybe the other person hasn't realized yet that you're ideal mates. Or maybe the relationship hasn't had time to "bake" and become a cohesive unit. It's still in batter form, and you're trying to serve it as cake. For every couple, the process of becoming a cohesive unit will be different. There isn't anyone who can tell you *exactly* where your relationship is in this process. You'll have to have faith and patience, and trust your intuition while you're going through the stages of a relationship. However, if you don't understand and recognize the stages, you won't be able to identify which one you're in! You'll even be more likely to sabotage your relationship because you're acting as if your relationship has progressed further than it actually has. Both partners in the relationship have to be in agreement about its current stage. For example, if after your first date you think you've met the woman you're going to marry and she still doesn't know if she wants to go on a second date, it's not the time to propose. It's not that you're wrong; it's that she may have to catch up to where you are in the relationship. You can't force someone to reach a stage in the relationship faster than they're ready to. In fact, trying to force someone to move faster than they're ready to may actually slow down the process.

In *Mars and Venus on a Date*, John Gray defined the five stages of dating as attraction, uncertainty, exclusivity, intimacy, and engagement. I'd like to share my views on these stages.

Stage One: Attraction

This is when you meet someone and bond with them physically, spiritually, emotionally, or mentally. You've done your preparation work. You recognize that the person has many qualities that are on your needs/wants list. You know you want to get to know them better.

Attraction at some level happens instantaneously. With rare exceptions your ideal mate will be someone with whom you've bonded (on some level) during the first stage.

Sometimes we may focus too much on only the physical aspects of a relationship when we're in the attraction stage. It's important to find out if you're attracted also to the person's mind, how they respond to life emotionally, and how they incorporate spirituality into their life. Ultimately, you want a *holistic* relationship, which is a combination of physical, emotional, mental, and spiritual bonding.

Remember, attraction is only the *first stage* in any relationship. It's when you're flirting, and smiling at the sound of their voice. It's when their mere *presence* makes you feel loving, happier, and euphoric. It's the honeymoon phase of a relationship. But it's *not* engagement. You don't have a commitment, so even though you bond and have a great time together, your expectations of someone you're *attracted* to may *not* be the same as those of someone you're *married* to.

Stage Two: Uncertainty

This is when the relationship dance begins. You realize that you may have met "the one." You start to question compatibility. You may think, "If only he would change this or that, he'd be perfect." Unfortunately, your fears about relationships begin showing up, whether you've summoned them or not.

You may feel that if everything isn't perfect, if it's not exactly what you visualized or believed it would be, then this isn't the relationship for you. But remember: as suggested in "Law of Preparation and Attraction," you list everything you want in a relationship but then let go of your expectations regarding the outcome. Someone isn't going to be *exactly* everything we want them to be, because we're all human. We may ask for perfection, but we have to realize that perfection is different for each person. Even soulmates will have a different definition of perfection. The purpose of coming together is to learn to love each other *despite* our flaws and to grow *past* them. In the uncertainty stage, we may have a tendency to think we should leave because of these flaws, but that's just a normal part of the process that ultimately makes the relationship cohesive.

Some couples may spend lots of time in uncertainty, while others fly right through it. You may even have to go back to attraction from time to time. Remember, each relationship is unique, and as we begin to see the flawed side of our prospective ideal mate, we may naturally feel uncertain about the relationship and where it should go.

The uncertainty stage is also about addressing our fears about relationships. Remember, we attract what we *actually* believe, not just what we *think* we believe. So, when you're feeling uncertain, pick up the mirror instead of the magnifying glass, because that will help you get through this stage. By recognizing your *own* concerns, you'll be able to grow and mirror that in the relationship.

Stage Three: Exclusivity

You've moved through uncertainty and are now seeing each other exclusively. You're both questioning whether or not this person really is your ideal mate, and you want to give the relationship a chance to grow without the influences of outside romantic interests. Remember, you aren't in an exclusive relationship until *both* people want it to be exclusive and verbally agree to it. *Never* assume you're exclusive until it's been discussed.

Don't confuse *exclusive* with *engaged*. It's not the time to start making wedding plans. It just means that you've agreed not to date other people. The exclusive stage is when you actually put the relationship cake in the oven. In stage one, you bought the ingredients and decided what type of cake to make. In stage two, you actually mixed the ingredients together. And now you've decided to see how the recipe tastes, so you've poured it in the pan and put it in the oven. You still don't know whether it'll bake, come out of the pan in good shape, and be edible or you'll need to work on the recipe some more. But you're willing to take the risk to find out.

This isn't the time to start being lazy in the relationship or to make unrealistic demands on your partner. You're still deciding if the relationship is something you want to pursue. It's a time for you and your partner to create loving romantic memories that allow you to feel good about yourself and the relationship. You'll need them when your fears about relationships surface and you're being tested either by yourself or by your partner.

Even after you've decided to see someone exclusively, you may find yourself backsliding into uncertainty. If your potential partner brings out wounds that you haven't healed, or inflicts new ones, you may begin to question the foundation and possibilities of the relationship. This is normal. Remember, your potential partner will be experiencing the same thing.

Although you've prepared to the best of your ability to be in a relationship and you really want to participate in one, you'll still have to become accustomed to actually being part of a couple. For example, you've always wanted to learn to tango. You've read books, watched videos, and practiced the steps in your living room, but there was only one problem: you were doing it *alone*. Finally, you meet someone who's also been practicing the tango alone and is looking for a partner. You're both eager to tango together. Although each of you has an understanding of the steps and the rhythm of the music, and has been practicing alone, you'll probably step on each other's feet a few times until you adjust to dancing together. You're actually going to have to practice with a partner to get in sync with the music. Relationships are the same way. In the exclusivity stage you start practicing the relationship dance as a unit. Of course, some couples pick up the steps quicker than others, but with practice lots of couples survive the exclusivity dance and move to intimacy.

Stage Four: Intimacy

You've been experiencing attraction to your partner on the physical, spiritual, emotional, and mental levels. With the intimacy stage, you actually begin to let these levels intertwine to create a holistic relationship. This is when real love begins to flourish.

You're not just focusing on the physical attraction, emotional feelings, mental stimulation, or spiritual connection. Now they're all *uniting* and *bonding* to become *one.*

You might think this is when a relationship becomes easier because love will flow between the partners in abundance. But it's also when we're the most vulnerable. During the first three stages we've appropriately maintained some emotional walls to protect ourselves from getting too hurt in the event the relationship doesn't work out.

During this intimacy stage, you each start letting go of some of the protective boundaries so you can really get to know each other in a nonprotective, emotionally wall-less environment, and you're opening the door for all of your fears about relationships to enter the picture. The biggest fear is that the other person will leave or in some other way choose to hurt us. Sometimes the feelings around holistic intimacy will be so intense at all levels that both people get scared and begin acting out. A man may go into his cave, and a woman will seem emotionally needy.

Just recognize that it's a normal part of the process, and don't run from it. With honest, strong communication, two people who've reached the intimacy stage can work through these fears. It does require your being honest about what you're feeling and not projecting it to your partner. Projecting is what happens when your mother says, "I'm cold; you need to wear a sweater." Your mother is projecting her needs, assuming they're yours. Another example: your fear of getting close to someone because you don't want to get hurt leads you to assume that your boyfriend's aloofness has its roots in a fear of getting too close to someone to avoid getting hurt. This may or may not be his reason for aloofness; he just may have been busy thinking about which new car to buy for the last month and didn't pay attention to relationship.

This stage of dating will begin bringing out the best and worst traits in both people. Your trust and faith in the process, yourself, and each other will be tested. It's the beginning of building the foundation for your lifetime relationship. In this stage you'll really determine if this is your ideal mate.

Recognize that holistic intimacy is scary for *everyone*. Remember to love yourself and your partner as you move through this critical stage of relationship building.

Stage Five: Engagement

You've each decided that you want to spend the rest of your lives together. You've found your soulmate. This will be one of the best times in your relationship. You're in love and feeling secure. You should take this time to create romantic memories that will help sustain you as you go through future times, in your marriage, that seem less romantic and more challenging.

During the engagement stage, you adjust to going from an "I" to a "we." Your thinking may already be at a "we" stage, since that develops during the first four stages of dating. However, we're each individuals and have a need to maintain our own identity. It may take longer for your beliefs to adjust to the concept of going from an "I" to a "we." But once you become engaged, you begin the process of merging two individuals into a "we."

Your decisions affect not only *you*, but your mate and the family you decide to create together. Your life isn't just about *your* wants and needs any longer; it's about you, your mate, and the life you've agreed to share together.

Don't shortchange the engagement process. It's when your "we" thinking becomes part of your belief system. It can be wonderful and romantic. It may even have moments of indecision and fear. The fact that you're engaged doesn't mean you'll escape the normal emotions and experiences of being human, but you're in the very best place to transcend your fears and bounce back to a state of love.

It's essential to recognize that all relationships have their own development time line. One couple may need to be in the exclusivity stage for three years, while another may become engaged after knowing each other for only six weeks. It's not about chronological time; it's about understanding the importance of allowing yourself and your partner to experience each stage of dating at a pace you're each comfortable with. If either partner tries to push the other through a stage that they aren't ready for, then you'll eventually end up having to repeat it in some way. It'll be more difficult for both of you than just having the patience to let the relationship progress at its natural pace. Also, think back to the Law of Mirroring: if your potential partner isn't ready to progress, what *belief* of yours are they mirroring? It may not be obvious. Beliefs sometimes hide but are always truthful. You may have to really sort through your emotional suitcase, but if you do you may get the change you want in the relationship.

Going through the stages of dating is laying the foundation for your house of love. You don't want to bypass or ignore a stage just because you're in a hurry. Have you ever decided to take a shortcut when you were putting something together, only to have to redo it, so that it took longer than if you'd done it right in the first place? Have you ever taken the time and energy to make plans for a group of people, only to find out that the whole group didn't want to do what you planned? When I think of craftsmanship, I think of Navajo rugs. They're each handwoven, the yarns all dyed by natural plants, and they take months or years to make, depending on the size, but they're all guaranteed to last a lifetime. Your relationship with your ideal mate is the most important thing you'll ever create. Take the appropriate amount of time for you and your mate to go through all of the stages of dating. Loving relationships take the time and commitment of two people to develop and can't be rushed. By laying the best foundation possible and avoiding shortcuts, you'll be creating a relationship that can last a lifetime.

The Three C's: Communication, Courtesy, Compassion

Love is what you've been through with somebody.
JAMES THURBER

Communication

Comunication is the most important tool you'll need to build and maintain your ideal relationship. Communication must first begin with yourself. You must be able to adequately determine what you really need and want in the relationship. Your needs/wants list is a great place to start, but you may find that as you experience the relationship, your needs and wants can change to reflect what's actually happening at the moment. For example, if you've had a long, exhausting week and you just want to be in the company of your significant other because they make you feel good, but you call and say, "I'd really like to see you because I want to tell you about what's going on, and how exhausted and overwhelmed I'm feeling," from your significant other's point of view this may sound draining, and they may be thinking, "I'd like to be supportive, but I'm also exhausted and I'm not sure I have anything to give." Your *real* need is their presence, but you communicated a laundry list that may have sounded exhausting. Before asking for something, be clear with yourself about exactly what you really want and how best to communicate it.

Communication is always tricky. There's no question that men and women communicate differently. If a man is feeling overwhelmed, depressed, or just doesn't know the answer to something, like how he feels, he'll hide in his cave. If a woman is experiencing the same things, she'll want to share and process her feelings with the people closest to her. Men think in terms of *tasks*, and women think in terms of *feelings*. This is basic emotional biology and internal wiring, so it's *not* going to change. It's like asking a dog to meow or a cat to bark; it's not going to happen, despite our altruistic reasons for asking. We can try to understand the differences and build bridges with our potential mates so that each person is more comfortable. The bridge you built in your last relationship will probably be different from the one you'll need to build in your current relationship. Everyone is different, and what worked once might not work in the current situation.

Remember, communication is a twofold process. It's about knowing and understanding your needs, and then being able to state them effectively. But it's also about listening to the other person. If you aren't listening, then you can't understand what they are saying. If you aren't listening, you may assume things about your partner's feelings that aren't true. When in doubt, clarify by asking questions. If you use humor you can usually get away with asking a lot of things, even before you reach the appropriate dating stage.

Communication in any relationship starts when we begin the dating process. It begins at the attraction stage. Since everyone has different styles of communication, it may take a while to figure out the exact style of someone you're attracted to. Some people are so direct they may be considered insensitive, while others may be so passive that they seem manipulative. Everyone communicates either directly or indirectly. For example, if you ask Lisa, "Would you like to eat Italian food?" a direct response would be, "I had Italian food for lunch. Can we get something else?" An indirect response would be, "I guess I can have Italian food twice in one day." Both responses mean the same thing, but the indirect response requires interpretation.

When you start dating, you set the tone for what type of communication you're willing to accept. For instance, you've met someone you're attracted to, they tell you they're going to call and make plans, but they never do. If, when you see them, you act excited and agree to go out if they call you, and never mention, even humorously, that they've done this before, you're sending a message that their noncommittal communication style is acceptable. If the relationship ever progresses to dating, you've already established a precedent for this ineffective type of communication to continue. If you want it to change (and that may not be possible because of the other person's character), you'll have to be honest about your feelings and discuss the fact that it bothers you. The good news would be either that it isn't their normal communication style or that they are willing to try and meet your need. The bad news would be that they do this all the time and don't understand that it's not acceptable, or that they promise to try to change this but never do. On the other hand, if you're an in-the-moment person and it doesn't bother you that someone says they're going to call and then doesn't, this could be your ideal mate.

As you go through the dating process you'll begin to communicate more and more. If you notice differences in your lifestyle, it's important to discuss them as they come up. The goal is *not* to get someone to change, but to determine if this person is *compatible* with you. Dating is about learning about people through repeated experiences. As you move through the stages of dating, question anything that doesn't feel right about the relationship. Just keep in mind that your questions should be appropriate to the stage of dating you're in.

For instance, when you're at the uncertainty stage, it's not the time to discuss whether your potential ideal mate is interested in having a large wedding or wants to elope. You may even want and hope your potential ideal mate will act a certain way, like calling you every day or seeing you every weekend. But it's not the time to discuss why he or she isn't doing what you want them to, because the action you want isn't appropriate for this early stage of the relationship.

However, once you move to exclusivity, you *can* ask more questions. For example, if you realize that your potential ideal mate leaves dirty dishes in the sink for days and this drives you nuts, this is the time to discuss the problem and begin looking to find out if a compromise exists. Once you find yourself engaged or married, it's unrealistic to think your mate will change and become a neat nut out of love for you. It's during the time that you're dating and getting to know each other that you have an opportunity to address lifestyle compatibility issues, before they become the make-it-or-break-it point of the relationship. Once you're moving into the intimacy and engagement stages, it's more difficult to admit someone isn't right for you and to let go and move forward. Dating isn't about trying to find fault with others. It's about finding the other puzzle piece that fits with you.

Despite good communication, most people's basic character traits and habits don't change. You can find compromises and solutions, but if you're counting on the other person changing in order for the relationship to work, your expectations may be too high. Soulmate relationships can provide the security for people to make changes, but the person who needs to change has to be the one who wants to make the change. You can love, support, and cheer them on, but you can't force change on someone. Changes are hard enough to make when you want to make them. Again, by going through the stages of dating at a pace that each person is comfortable with, each person will have time to try to make changes in the confines of a safe relationship and find out if they can actually live with the changes.

Communication isn't only about what you *say*. It's also what you *do*. In fact, some language experts say as much as 70 percent of communication is nonverbal. So, if you agree to do something for your ideal mate and don't do it, it'll begin to chip away at your partner's trust. On the other hand, if you keep your word, you build trust with every action. Nonverbal communication is expressed by the tone of your voice, doing a kind deed, or giving a hug. Never underestimate the power of nonverbal expressions of love.

Communication is the only way you'll ever be able to work through your problems and share your victories. Your key to understanding and sharing in your ideal mate's life, and developing the relationship you both want, is your willingness to develop and build all of your communication skills.

Courtesy

Once you've met the person you believe is your ideal mate, you often expect that person to react in certain ways. You think they're supposed to be your everything. Now, if you created a whole, balanced life while you were in the process of manifesting your mate, this will be less of a problem because you have other things in your life that meet your needs. But once you begin expecting certain behaviors from someone, you often forget to be courteous and grateful, and tend to focus on expectations that aren't being fulfilled instead of the positive things that are happening.

If you're at the exclusivity stage, you may *expect* someone to attend your mother's birthday party. But inviting the person to attend and expecting them to are two entirely different things. In fact, family obligations may or may not be a part of your relationship, depending on your individual backgrounds and beliefs. Being courteous is about respecting your potential ideal mate's rights to either want or not want to do something, including attending your mother's birthday party. So, invite—but don't *expect*.

Courtesy is remembering to express your gratitude and appreciation when your potential ideal mate does things that make you feel good or helps you out. Sometimes it's just being grateful they gave you a hug, said a kind word, or smiled. If you get in the habit of focusing on being courteous when you're dating, it'll be easier to keep doing it throughout the life of your relationship. Everyone wants to feel appreciated whether they've been in the relationship one month, one year, or twenty-five years.

Being courteous means recognizing that although you have news that you want to share, it may not be the best time for your ideal mate to hear it. For example, if you just got a job promotion and you called your best girlfriend to tell her, and she immediately told you that her father was in the hospital, in all probability you'd listen to your friend, be supportive, and wait until a more appropriate time to share your news. But with our potential ideal mates, we often think that they should be just as excited or upset as we are about something, despite what's going on in their life, and we go ahead and share even if it's not considerate of the space they're in. They may just want to sit, relax, and watch a basketball game or movie. Being courteous is recognizing other people have needs that may not match yours at every moment and respecting that.

Some people are more considerate of their pets than they are of their mates. I know your cat can't argue with, hurt, or leave you, but despite the fact you've told it a million times to quit climbing on the kitchen counter, you realize and accept that it's not going to happen. You don't get mad at the cat every time it climbs on the kitchen counter. There will be some habits and traits that your ideal mate has that you don't like but can live with, so you'll need to apply the same rule of acceptance to them that you would to your pet. Consideration is about loving people *despite* their imperfections.

Compassion

When you're in a relationship with a prospective ideal mate, not only will it bring up great feelings of love, but it will magnify your fears. When we're feeling fearful, even for brief moments, we have a tendency to act out inappropriately. It's important that you recognize that if you're experiencing these strong feelings, your potential ideal mate may be experiencing the same thing. You may react differently but feel similar emotions. Therefore, you need to be compassionate when either one of you makes mistakes.

Everyone is human and will make mistakes while participating in a journey with another person. It's important to recognize that most people aren't intentionally trying to hurt you. Compatibility may be an issue, but if you know you're compatible, then when someone appears to be inconsiderate, it's probably because they're dealing with one of their own demons. Most likely it has nothing to do with *you* directly. For example, maybe your potential ideal mate has a pending job change coming up at work. You may not know about the stressful situation, but when you suggest making plans for a vacation and they don't comment or seem interested, you feel ignored. Your potential mate does not want to share information about this stressful situation right now, but you take their lack of response as a personal rejection, when in reality your partner may not even know if they can take time off from work for a vacation, or even if they'll have a job.

Compassion is about giving someone the temporary benefit of the doubt when you're feeling frustrated. It's a gift partners give to each other in order for their relationship to survive the challenges all relationships must go through. It doesn't mean that you just ignore the situation, but you may pick and choose when you're going to address it. Sometimes time is the real healer and the problem will work itself out without any help from you.

Compassion is about being selfless toward another for the benefit of the relationship. It's *not* about being a martyr. It's about giving an emotional gift and trusting it'll be returned when you need it.

Having good communication, being courteous, and showing compassion are all critical when you're building an ideal relationship. They're skills that when developed and applied will enable you to experience a lifetime romance with your ideal mate.

When Suzie was planning her wedding she asked her grandmother how she and her grandfather managed to keep their marriage happy for more than fifty years.

Her grandmother responded, "On the day we got married, I told myself that I would always forgive him for ten things he did that annoyed me. In fact, I'd never mention them to him."

Suzie asked, "How did you decide what was going to be on the list?"

Her grandmother responded, "Oh, I never actually wrote anything down. I just assumed, when he did something that annoyed me, it was on the list."

Soulmates: Reflecting Love and Magnifying Fear

Love doesn't make the world go 'round. Love is what makes the ride worthwhile.
AUDREY WOODHALL

Obstacles are those frightful things you see when you take your eyes off the goal.
HANNAH MOORE

Think back to the Law of Mirroring: you recognize in other people the very emotions and traits that you're working on in yourself. When you meet a soulmate the Law of Mirroring is magnified beyond normal. You'll feel love at a more intense level, as well as fear and any other emotional issues that you share. It's important that you be aware of your feelings and acknowledge them first to yourself and then at the appropriate time to your potential mate.

To help you overcome the magnified fears of relationships, in *Two Hearts Are Better Than One* Bob Mandel describes a game that helps open up the lines of communication between partners. Each partner simply states everything that they're fearful of about relationships and members of the opposite sex. For example: "Men are controlling," "Women are manipulative," "I'll lose my identity," "I'll lose my freedom." The challenge is, you can't correct or argue against anything that your partner says. You simply agree with them. The purpose is to allow each of you to put all of your fear cards on the table. Expressing your fear-based ideas and feelings about relationships allows you to begin releasing them from your subconscious. I like to add another part to the game: after you've expressed all of your fears, state all of the things you believe or want a loving relationship to include. This starts reprogramming your subconscious to create the relationship you both want. This exercise is best done as you enter the exclusivity or the intimacy stage of dating.

"Love is walking through fear," says Rokelle Lerner, a nationally known speaker, therapist, and relationship expert. When you're in love, it gives you the key to open up the closets that you keep your fears hidden in. Of course, when you open those doors you have the opportunity to clean out those closets and replace your fears with loving experiences.

The emotional experiences you share with your soulmate are just an extension of the infinite well of emotions you have within you. Soulmates are just the people who give us the opportunity to learn to recognize and express them.

Relationship Goals

You seldom get what you go after unless you know in advance what you want.
MAURICE SWITZER

When your relationship moves into the exclusivity and intimacy stages, you'll want to start discussing your short- and long-term relationship goals. During the getting-to-know-you dating phases of attraction and uncertainty, you probably found out a few things, such as if he's committed to staying a bachelor or that she doesn't want children. If you find these things are a problem, you shouldn't have progressed to the exclusivity and intimacy stages of dating. Remember, dating *isn't* about changing another person; it's about *choosing to grow together.*

When you're in the exclusivity stage you'll start setting short-term goals, like planning trips, taking classes, or entertaining your friends together. Doing these things will show how you work together on a common goal that's nonthreatening, and that knowledge will help you as you move into the intimacy stage of the relationship.

Once you reach the intimacy stage you'll start considering long-term goals. Do you want to live in a house or an apartment? How do you manage money? What are your ideas about family responsibility? Look at your needs/wants list, and begin talking about the goals on your list. If your individual goals are compatible, you may start setting goals together as your relationship grows. Once you set a goal, start working toward it. Become a team.

Once you've become engaged you'll obviously have the goal of planning a wedding. But what will be your goals *after* the wedding? Do you want to start a family? Do you already have families that you'll be merging into one? Do you have career goals that might affect your mate? Do you want to retire when you're forty? Before you walk down the aisle, make sure you're honest and discuss your goals and create a plan for achieving them.

Throughout the course of your relationship you'll always be setting goals and revamping them, depending on circumstances. You'll have personal, professional, and family goals, but don't forget to prioritize your *relationship* goals. Setting goals gives you an opportunity to create memorable experiences while achieving something together and growing as individuals and as a couple.

Creating Win-Win Solutions

*Criticizing others is like shining a spotlight into their eyes;
then they can't see anything at all.*
ANONYMOUS

The real work begins once you've attracted your ideal mate. You're going to have to negotiate and compromise about some things in your relationship. No two people will agree on absolutely everything. This is why it's very important that you be clear about what you *need* and what you *want*—things you're *not willing* to negotiate and things that you're *willing* to negotiate.

If you've prepared yourself by repacking your emotional suitcase and you've been through all five stages of the dating relationship, both of you must realize that you'll each have to participate in the give-and-take process of relationships.

You can create win-win situations throughout the stages of the dating relationship, but each has to be appropriate to that stage of the relationship. When you're in the initial attraction stage, that's not the time to try to create a win-win situation about whether or not someone should call you every day. But it is the time to observe the communication styles and needs of the person you're attracted to.

Win-win situations are about finding solutions and letting go of the notion of who or what is *right*. In all likelihood, there isn't a right or wrong in most situations; there's just *different*. Win-win situations begin by simple negotiation.

Negotiating may sound unromantic, but it's the best way to find a win-win solution for things you and your partner disagree about. If the problem is a particularly big or sensitive one, then the first thing you have to do is schedule a specific time to discuss your problem. If it's small, like what to watch on TV, then it may take only a few minutes. If you need to schedule an appointment, do it when it's mutually convenient, not when one of you has an emotional need to explode or when someone is on a deadline. By setting a time, you will also have an opportunity to release your anger before negotiating the solution. You can't negotiate while you're feeling anger. Anger clings to individualism and the ego, making right and wrong the issue. Remember, you and your partner are on the *same* team and have a *common* goal, of *mutual* happiness. Drop your win-lose attitude about negotiating when it comes to your lover: you want to create win-win situations.

When you have your discussion, it's important that each of you have the opportunity to state your side of the problem or issue and how you feel about it. The conversation should be only about issues relative to the problem. Keep the rest of your emotional suitcase closed. Recognize your needs and what you want. Determine how you can get your needs honored. By discussing the problem or issue in a nonemotional, solution-oriented manner, you can either find neutral ground for a compromise or determine why it's more important that things be done in one of the partner's ways. Maybe for one of you the issue is a want and for the other it's a need.

If you approach problems with an intent to create win-win solutions, one will not escape you. Your intent to create win-win opportunities opens the door for the Universe to give you win-win solutions.

For example, your relationship is at level four, intimacy. You have a need to participate in a couples' growth weekend. You want to spiritually bond more with your partner. You mention this to your partner, but they feel your spiritual relationship is fine and they're uncomfortable with the idea of going to a spiritual relationship weekend. It's not even on their want list. What's the solution? Perhaps initially going to an evening lecture about spirituality and relationships. If your partner is comfortable with that, maybe the next time you can go to a daylong workshop, and then eventually the full weekend. You'll be getting some of your needs met without putting your partner in a situation that they're resistant to.

Again, I'm assuming you're in a loving relationship with someone who has your best interests at heart, just as you have theirs at heart. If you're the only one making the compromises, then it's *not* a win-win solution. If your partner doesn't know how to negotiate, you may need to consider couples counseling. Depending on your relationship, counseling can be a necessary part of maintenance.

Win-win solutions are about making each person feel good about the outcome. It's not about feeling as if you lost or had to give up part of yourself or something you need, in order to make the relationship work. Win-win solutions *aren't* about what's right or wrong. They're about viewing your relationship needs as *equal* to your individual needs, living in a state of love.

Joan and Larry had a date. Larry's friend John was home on leave from Vietnam, and Larry asked if they could stop by to see John on their way to the movies.

"Fine," replied Joan, who had not really wanted to go out with Larry in the first place.

Two days later, John called Joan. She remembered that their first conversation was about how neither of them wanted to get married in the near future. She was eighteen and planning on going to school, and he was going back to Vietnam.

They saw each other every night for the next two weeks. It was more mental and emotional than romantic bonding. Joan recognized that there was more to the relationship than a whirlwind romance. It was very sweet, subtle, and quiet.

They corresponded for the next six months while John was in Vietnam. Their letters were their courtship, and they really got to know each other through them. Joan believed that they were building a future and would get married one day; she just didn't know when.

After John got back from Vietnam, it was like starting over. They had to go through the "Is this real and still right?" stage, but within a year John and Joan were married.

They've been married for twenty-six years and have two grown children. Joan says, "We've had to learn to let each of us be who we are individually. And also that sometimes you have to put your marriage first over your individual needs."

John has always had a lot of women friends through work. He always seemed to mentor women and help them get through the politics of a company. It was never lots of women at the same time, just different women at different points in his career. Early in their marriage Joan was uncomfortable with this, although she never felt any reason to be insecure.

Joan thinks John likes to help these women because his mother had low self-esteem. He seems to be on a spiritual mission to help them. Joan knew in her heart there wasn't anything more to these relationships than friendship and support, but still she struggled with a conflict within herself. One night one of these women and her boyfriend were over at their house for dinner. The woman's boyfriend was having the same insecure reaction Joan did, and Joan realized she didn't want to look like he did.

Joan realized she needed to discuss her feelings with John. John's response was, "What can I do to make you feel better?" Joan told him, and John agreed to change some of his behaviors.

Soon after that discussion, a woman who worked with John told Joan, "You have a very nice husband. Your husband is extremely respectful, unlike so many of the men we work with."

"I took that as God's way of telling me that everything was fine even when I wasn't there," Joan said.

Growing Through the Different Types of Love

Each small task of everyday life is part of the total harmony of the universe.
SAINT THÉRÈSE OF LISIEUX

My mind is my garden, my thoughts are my needs.
I will harvest either flowers or weeds.
ANONYMOUS

Whether you're in one of the earlier stages of a relationship with your potential ideal mate or you've reached the engagement stage or marriage, you'll be facing the challenges and rewards of maintaining the growth that's necessary for a healthy, holistic relationship. All relationships are like gardens: they need tending. If you pick out the weeds and water and fertilize your plants and they receive the proper amount of light, in most cases they grow and bloom. You reap the benefits of beautiful flowers and green leaves.

To achieve holistic love, you'll have to develop it at the physical, spiritual, mental, and emotional levels. In "Law of Love," we defined each of these types of love. Now we'll look at how you can share them in a mutually fulfilling relationship.

Physical love is expressed through touching, kissing, and making love. There's a difference between making love and having sex. "Having sex is the physical act of sharing pleasure with your partner," according to Barbara DeAngelis. "Making love is the emotional act of loving and adoring your partner."

It's true that you can have sex without making love, and make love without having sex. Of course, the best combination is having sex and making love at the same time. But as your relationship matures, there will be times that you may want *only* to have sex or *only* to make love.

You and your partner need to feel free to communicate this. Sometimes we feel that if we aren't making love, then love *isn't* involved. But that *isn't* true. You can have lusty feelings for someone you love. Sometimes you just may not feel like taking the time to have a romantic evening of lovemaking but would enjoy the physical expression of sex. Of course, if your partner never wants to make love and wants *only* to have sex, then you may have problems. By allowing yourself to express your sexual needs, you're opening the doors of communication and creating intimacy within the boundaries of your relationship.

Remember the power of touch when expressing your physical love. The energy in your hands can be used to express love not only during lovemaking and having sex, but throughout the day. Whenever possible, give your lover a loving pat on the back, stroke their arm or leg, or hold their hand. Give your partner lots of hugs, because they're an opportunity to share your loving energy. The way you're feeling emotionally—a loving, angry, or happy mood—will be shared with your partner when you touch. If you're angry, not even necessarily with your partner, then *that's* the energy that will be exchanged when you're hugging, holding hands, or making love. If you want your partner to feel loved, make sure you're in that emotional state when you touch them. By consistently and regularly expressing loving gestures, you're maintaining the emotional bonding necessary for your relationships to be in a state of making love all the time.

Take the time to enjoy romantic kisses during the course of the day, not just when you're having sex or making love. By sharing loving, lingering kisses throughout the day you're always participating in foreplay.

Expressing physical love isn't just about sharing sexual experiences; it's about showing, through your nonverbal communication, how much you love and care about someone all of the time. Expressing physical love in nonsexual ways will only heighten and strengthen your sexual experiences with your partner.

It's important to have open communication about your physical love needs in a safe environment. Some people may need more hugs, others may want more sex, and some may want to make love less often. In all relationships your expression of physical love will grow and change as each partner grows and changes. With open communication you'll be able to grow and share in the expression of physical love *together.*

Spiritual love is expressed by inviting God, or the universal force, into your relationship. It's recognizing that for your relationship to blossom and grow, you and your mate will need help from something with a divine connection. This is why most weddings are performed at a religious site, like a church, synagogue, temple, or mosque. You and your mate are sharing with your family and friends that you're not only welcoming but *inviting* God to help maintain your relationship.

Since spiritual love means recognizing that each person in the relationship has their own spiritual journey to complete, spiritual love includes asking for divine assistance to help keep both partners on the same path without interfering in their individual journeys. Some things can't be accomplished without divine intervention.

During the dating process it's important, especially as you move into the exclusivity and intimacy stages, to determine the role each of you wants God, or a universal power, to play in your relationship.

Some people actively practice their religion. Others are adamantly opposed to any form of organized religion but are highly spiritual. Some people believe meditation is their connection to God. Others have no interest in the spiritual. You'll need to know the role the issue will play in your relationship and how it will affect your current or future family.

Often we ignore establishing a connection to God regarding our relationships until there is a crisis, maybe an illness, accident, or death. Then, suddenly, we are looking for *answers* and need to find inner peace because we're aching inside. I strongly suggest that you establish a relationship with some spiritual source *before* a crisis happens, not because it'll help you avoid unpleasant situations but because when they do happen you will already believe that you have access to help from a universal power.

As you grow as a couple, there will be times when you question why you're together, even if you're soulmates. Relationships make our lives better, but they aren't easy. There aren't always simple solutions, but having the support of God always helps. Relationships that actively welcome spiritual growth by inviting the assistance of God are blessed.

Emotional love is the energy you feel when you're interacting with your mate, and it's expressed in every word and action you exchange with your partner. As your relationship grows and matures, this love should also become more confident and stable.

Practicing emotional love is about providing a safe space for each person to have the opportunity to express *all* of their feelings, including anger, rage, fear, sadness, joy, love, happiness, and ecstasy. It doesn't mean that one of you should be projecting their negative feelings to the other, or that anyone should ever accept being abused in the name of emotional love. Expressing how you feel isn't about projection, or assuming someone else perceives the experience from how you perceive it; it's about owning your feelings and working through the emotions. Emotional love in a relationship is just a safe, supportive place to do it.

You'll experience heightened levels of emotional intimacy when your relationship is a sanctuary in which you can own all of your feelings and share them with your partner while knowing you'll receive unconditional love. This will take practice. Some days it'll be easier than others. We're all human, and we all have an emotional suitcase. You'll be working through it more with your ideal mate than anyone else. This is when you'll have to practice the three C's: communication, courtesy, and compassion.

Mental love is sharing in intellectual stimulation with your partner. It's an intellectual energy that evokes thinking between you and your mate. You won't always have the same interests and expertise as your partner. They may know more about computers, and you may know more about car repairs. Mental love is respecting each person as capable of learning and having expertise in different areas.

Your mental love will be shared as you go through your journey together. When you have common experiences—buying a house, having children, planning for your retirement, learning new hobbies, finding new interests—you'll have opportunities to strengthen the mental love in your relationship.

If one of you is an expert in a particular area, the other person may want to take an interest in it and learn something about it so they can share in conversations. It's not about competing with your mate, but sharing in their interests.

Your partner can't and shouldn't be your *only* source of mental stimulation. You'll need to learn new things on your own throughout the life of your relationship so you'll have something to *share* with your partner. Conversation is part of the spice of life. Even if you and your partner don't have that many intellectual interests in common when you meet, you can easily add to them by looking for mutual interests. Bonding at the mental level is critical to cementing your holistic relationship.

Holistic love is active bonding at the physical, spiritual, emotional, and mental levels. This is the highest form of love you can experience personally and in any relationship. You have to be growing in each of the areas personally in order for the relationship to involve love at all of those levels. You can't bring something to your relationship that you don't have.

From time to time, your relationship will go through periods when it may not be growing in one area as much as in others. This is normal, but when you become aware of it, first look at yourself and make sure *you're* still growing in that area, then discuss it with your mate and see what you can do to change it. But don't panic. Look for solutions that begin with yourself and can extend into your relationship.

Maintaining a holistic love requires commitment and effort on the part of both partners. One partner can't be responsible for a whole relationship. Relationships are about *two* people who mutually agree to come together to share their lives. They aren't about *one* partner doing all of the work and making all of the changes.

A holistic relationship is a safe, loving environment in which you can continue your spiritual journey as an individual and share it with another person. It's actively expressing and receiving love at every level possible.

Byron and John met when they were working for the same charity. They were almost instantly attracted to each other and started spending time together, going to dinner and participating in the causes they both volunteered for.

Although they were very attracted to each other, their time was limited during their first few dates, and they didn't want their first intimate encounter to be a quickie. They chose to wait until they had the time to have a long romantic day. Byron explained that in gay relationships this isn't the normal pattern. By the time Byron and John actually became physically involved, they were already falling in love.

Within six weeks of meeting they knew they were life mates and moved in together. Their friends refer to them as the "artsy Ozzie and Harriet." They've been able to create a loving home that people feel comfortable in.

They both feel that their past relationships and experiences helped them understand the importance of commitment. They also knew what was important in a relationship and what their priorities were. Problems—which, oddly enough, usually weren't about their relationship but about things like family problems, health concerns, and career changes—were always addressed from a perspective of "we" instead of "I." There was a team attitude about what was best for the "us," not just the individual "me's."

They've been together for four years and are now in their early forties. They credit their great relationship to the fact that they bonded mentally, emotionally, and spiritually before bonding physically. They knew they liked and complemented each other, so they could easily move into a holistic relationship.

Relationship Cycles

The road to success has many tempting parking places.
STEVE POTTER

All relationships have cycles, just as your life has cycles. We all come into this world as babies and progress through the stages of being toddlers, children, teenagers, young adults, adults, midlife adults, and finally, mature adults. Fortunately, being a mature adult has come to be more about a state of mind than about chronological age, but we *still* progress. We have different experiences during those times of our lives.

Our relationships will be different depending on how many we've experienced, our stage of life, and what we want at the time of the relationship. Your first true love may happen when you're sixteen or sixty. The goals in your relationship will be different depending on whether you're first-time newlyweds, raising children, or retired. These experiences will affect how you'll relate to each other.

For instance, when you've just had a baby and you're not getting any sleep, you may not feel sexy and romantic. Your partner probably isn't getting much sleep either and may be feeling the same way. You wanted to be a parent and are excited about having the baby, but it'll definitely be a new cycle in your relationship. You'll have to make a point to find time to share your physical love. Some people will shortchange this part of their lives when their children arrive, but you shouldn't do that. In order to experience holistic love you have to practice physical, emotional, mental, and spiritual bonding with your partner throughout the entire life of your relationship.

Also, when either you or your partner is going through a personal growth experience it can affect the cycle of your relationship. Some personal growth experiences that affect relationships are losing a parent, a major career change (positive or negative), experiencing disease, and needing a change in your spiritual connection to God. If you aren't content with yourself, you can't fully share in the relationship, because you can't give something you don't have, even if you're soulmates and lifelong partners. Each person has to be wise enough to recognize when their mate needs a little compassion and to see that they'll be more participatory in the relationship as soon as they've completed their personal growth experience. Although the personal growth experience of your mate affects you, it's not *about* you. When discussing communication goals, try having an agreement that each person will announce if they're going through something even if they don't want to share it. That way the other partner isn't in the dark.

Even when you're with your soulmate, every experience is not about *both* of you. You're still two individuals who've agreed to come together to share your lives. This means you have to practice spiritual love from time to time and let your partner fly and learn to do things on their own. If your partner doesn't share for extended periods of time, then you may need professional help to get you through the cycle.

Some of the cycles will be positive. You'll feel like your life is raining roses. Positive relationship cycles include falling in love, engagement, your wedding day, being newlyweds, buying your first home, becoming parents, sending your children off to college, and becoming grandparents. But you'll notice that even the positive experiences can include stress. Stress happens for individuals and the relationship during both positive and negative cycles.

Commitment to the positive growth of each individual and of the relationship is crucial to get through both the positive and the negative cycles of relationships. Without commitment, when things get stressful you may want to leave. Commitment will give you the strength to let go when necessary and to persevere despite obstacles. Relationships are about choices. Making a commitment is the *choice* to stay through all of the cycles of a relationship, including the good, bad, ugly, and better than anything you could ever imagine.

Wayne's friend Keith and Janet's sister Barbara were going to set them up on a blind date. Wayne had been burned on a few blind dates, so he decided to check Janet out before agreeing to go.

Janet worked at the local Dairy Queen, so one June afternoon Wayne drove through to get a soda and peek at Janet. It was love at first sight for Wayne. That night he stopped by Janet's house to meet her. Janet and Wayne seemed to fit together from the moment they met. The following Saturday they had their first movie date, and one week later Wayne was off to boot camp. Janet wasn't too happy about this and said she wouldn't have gone out with him on even one date if she'd known. But she really liked him, so she wrote him anyway. When he returned, the relationship resumed, and Wayne proposed that September. Janet knew she wanted to marry Wayne, but she didn't want to be engaged while he was overseas. She'd heard too many stories of military men going away, only to break up with their fiancées because they met some-one new.

Wayne was persistent. In December, he proposed again and wanted to give Janet a ring. She again wanted to wait, but by her birthday, in January, she accepted. In March, Wayne went overseas for fourteen months.

During this time they seemed to cultivate their psychic link to each other. Janet would dream of things that were happening on the ship Wayne was on and write to him about it. He'd be shocked that she knew what was going on.

Wayne came home on an emergency leave when his father needed heart surgery. During the month he was home, he and Janet were married.

Things went reasonably well for the first five years. But then, both agree, Wayne entered a selfish phase. He wasn't paying any attention to Janet or helping with the new baby. Janet was working days, and Wayne was working nights. They didn't seem to have any time to be together.

One day when they were driving to Austin to visit relatives for the week-

end, they heard a man on the radio discussing the Edgar Cayce teachings. Everything he said hit a cord for both Janet and Wayne. Upon returning home they immediately began studying the Edgar Cayce teachings.

That spiritual journey became the foundation for their growth as individuals and a couple. It was what helped them solidify a holistic relationship.

One of the philosophies that they credit for helping them handle problems in their marriage and life is expressed in the Prayer of Indifference: "He or she is divine, just as I'm divine. Do that which will bring peace and harmony between us."

Janet and Wayne have been married for twenty-eight years. Their marriage has seen two children grow up, their parents pass away, and the blessing of two grandchildren. They've always made time for dates, and they make an effort to communicate their needs and be respectful and loving toward each other.

Looking back, they both realize that from the moment they met, divine intervention has played a part in their lives. Their psychic bond has often helped them understand what the other person is feeling and experiencing. They recognized the importance of universal coincidence and of having faith and patience, which allows them to develop a loving relationship.

Twenty Things to Maintain the Love in Your Relationship

Kindness in words creates confidence. Kindness in thinking creates profoundness. Kindness in giving creates love.
LAO-TZU

You've met your ideal mate. You think life will be grand forever. And it will, for a few moments, and maybe lots of them. But you can't ignore the maintenance that keeps it grand, that keeps love and romance alive in your relationship. Some of your relationship cycles will be less loving and romantic than others, so I've included some things you can do to help keep love in your relationship all of the time.

1. Say "I love you" at least once a day.
2. Passionately kiss your partner (other than during foreplay) at least three times a day.
3. Leave love notes in your partner's car and briefcase and on the mirror.
4. Go on a date, just the two of you, once a week or every other week.
5. Plan a romantic getaway for a day, weekend, or week.
6. Go on a surprise picnic.
7. Learn something about your partner's favorite hobby so you can talk about it.

8. Learn a few romantic phrases in a romantic language like Spanish, French, or Italian.
9. Take a candlelit bath together.
10. Give your partner a relaxing, nonsexual massage.
11. Send a flirtatious message to your mate through E-mail.
12. Have a "clothing optional" dinner party for yourself and your mate.
13. Send flowers just because.
14. Call to say "Hi."
15. Mail your partner a romantic greeting card.
16. Tell your partner one thing you appreciate about them at least once a day.
17. Never assume that your partner will do something. Always have the respect and courtesy to *ask.*
18. Read an erotic novel together.
19. Go dancing.
20. Take a walk under the stars.

The Law of Maintenance is about recognizing where you are in the relationship and acting accordingly. Maintenance is never easy, but it doesn't have to be painful. Preventive maintenance is always better than actually having to repair something that's broken.

Each relationship is unique and has special maintenance requirements. You may make what feels like a few mistakes while trying to recognize what maintenance needs to be done in your relationship, so be patient and loving with yourself. Your mate will be having the same challenges. Also, as the relationship grows and changes, the maintenance will change.

Every action, thought, and communication on the part of either you or your mate will affect the maintenance needs of your relationship. When you agree to unite and share your lives, you become a team. Teams require the cooperation of all the players in an effort to reach the same goal.

With proper maintenance your relationship will survive all its highs and lows, and you'll experience more soul growth and love than you've ever imagined possible. Your relationship is a blessing from God, so cherish *all* of the moments it brings into your life.

Two hearts are better than one.

BOB MANDEL

Part Four

❧

Law of
Letting Go

Some of God's greatest gifts are unanswered prayers.
GARTH BROOKS, "UNANSWERED PRAYERS"

When one door closes another opens. Expect new doors to reveal even greater wonders, glories and surprises.
EILEEN CADDY

How many times have you prayed that God would make someone yours? If he answered this one prayer, you wouldn't ask for anything ever again. In Garth Brooks's hit song "Unanswered Prayers," he tells a story of seeing his first love at a high school football game many years later. He introduces her to his wife. He thinks about his past, when he hoped and prayed the relationship with the first love would last forever. Upon seeing her again years later, he realizes his wife is a gift in his life. He then thanks God for not answering his prayers years earlier, because if God had, he wouldn't be married to his wife. When you feel that something isn't working out that you're hoping and praying for, remember: you may not be aware of what's around the corner for you. A friend of mine would always tell me, "If the relationship you're in doesn't work out, it's because God has a better one for you."

Now, when you're in the middle of having to let someone you love go, this isn't what you want to hear—even if it's true. Take a moment and write down a couple of examples of when you really wanted something, didn't get it, and were unaware something better was around the corner. For example, you thought you wanted a promotion in a different department at your company. You applied, interviewed, and thought you would be the perfect candidate. But you didn't get the promotion. Two months later that position was eliminated. Shortly after, you received a promotion in *your* department. When you didn't get the first promotion, you may have been feeling rejected and angry. But hindsight being 20/20, was your prayer really unanswered, or did you actually dodge a bullet? Keep the list in a place where you can easily read it when you're feeling that God isn't listening. It'll remind you of times when your unanswered prayers were gifts.

When you're feeling lonely or hurting, it's easy to get mad at God. You may think your prayers are being ignored if you feel the only piece missing in your life is the perfect mate and that person hasn't arrived. This is particularly true when you've been in a relationship that you believed had great potential. You invested time, energy, and love in another person, only to find out the feelings weren't mutual or that this was a stepping-stone relationship. One way to limit your frustration is to limit the amount of time you spend in a relationship that isn't meant to be lifelong.

Signs That a Relationship Isn't Working

You never know what is enough until you know what is more than enough.
WILLIAM BLAKE

We've all been at that crossroads in relationship land where we're trying to make a choice about whether we should stay and try to work things out or cut our losses, let go, and move forward. Relationships with people remind me of relationships with cars. When you buy a new one, it's exciting. You promise to go to great efforts to take care of it and keep it looking and smelling new. The longer you own the car, the more you'll have to do. You may have to change filters, belts, hoses, or tires, and get tune-ups; and occasionally a battery or the air conditioner has to be replaced. With the proper care and maintenance, your car may last for many more miles than you could imagine. But what about when you get the new car that's a lemon? It's in the shop every week for more than the ten-minute oil change. Eventually you'll get tired of dealing with the hassle and trade it in for a better car.

All relationships will require a normal amount of maintenance. Sometimes they may need more than the quick ten minutes of bonding time. That's part of individual and relationship growth. However, there are some signs that a relationship is a lemon and you should cut your losses and trade it in for a new model. Your lesson may very well be along the lines of "Just say no." If you don't love yourself enough to have healthy boundaries, no one else will do it for you.

Lemon Relationship Warning Signs

- *Your intuition (not your fears) tells you something isn't right*

  You have a gut feeling that something in the relationship isn't right. You may not have the facts to back up your feelings, but your instincts are the best gauge of whether or not this is a fit for you. In all probability, if your intuition is telling you something is wrong—it's right. Your intuition wouldn't send you the "Something's wrong" signals and expect you to repair the other person. Your intuition is there to protect *you,* not fix other people.

- *You have different values*

  Values include things like honesty, work ethics, and spiritual beliefs. You feel planning for the future is important, and your potential mate is an in-the-moment person. Of course, you must have a clear understanding of your own values before you'll know if you have different values.

- *Poor communication*

  You feel you're always having to pull information from your partner. You're having to guess what they're thinking. Their verbal words and nonverbal actions don't match. For example, your prospective mate tells you on Wednesday, "We should go to the movies on Saturday." Saturday comes and goes, and you haven't heard a word.

- *One person cares more than the other person*

  We've all been there. One person in the relationship thinks the other person walks on water. But the feeling isn't mutual.

- *Unavailability, physical or emotional*

  Obviously (except in *extremely* rare karmic relationships) if the person you're dating is married, engaged, or dating several other people, there's a physical unavailability and a lemon sign on the relationship. But don't forget emotional unavailability. For example, if your potential mate is thirty and still hates the opposite sex because their heart was broken at nineteen by their first love, you're dealing with someone who's emotionally guarded and unavailable to be with you. If by this point in their life they can't let go of their past hurt and love again, it's unlikely you're their relationship healer. People have to want to heal, and ultimately they have to heal themselves.

- *Lack of compatibility on a physical, emotional, mental, or spiritual level*

   Love isn't everything. You must also be compatible. If you aren't, then instead of enjoying the relationship moments, you'll be putting your energy and efforts into trying to get your potential mate to do it your way. Compatibility doesn't mean that you'll never have to compromise or negotiate, but you shouldn't have to give up the things that are most important to you.

- *Attraction to what is only potential*

   If you're dating someone about whom you're constantly thinking, "With my help this person can reach their full potential and be someone they haven't even dreamed they'd want to be," then you're more attracted to their potential than to who they actually are. You'll end up spending your time and energy thinking, "If I just love them enough and am patient, then they'll learn to spread their wings and fly," instead of actually participating in and enjoying the relationship.

Pay attention to the lemon warning signs. If you're spending more time maintaining the relationship than enjoying the ride, then you need to evaluate your relationship and determine if it's the one for you.

You may realize after a few dates, weeks, months, or even years that you're in a relationship that isn't the "until death us do part" one. You then become aware you'll have to endure the experience of letting go.

Since everyone and every relationship is unique, the experience of letting go will be unique to that situation. However, the one thing the letting-go process has in common for everyone at some point is that you'll have to experience the five stages of grief: denial, bargaining, anger, depression, and finally acceptance.

Someone who has been married for a long time and then suddenly finds themselves single may have an easier time letting the relationship go than someone who dated their potential ideal mate for only a few months. It just depends on the experiences that took place during the life of the relationship. If you were married, you may have already experienced much of the grieving process during the life of the marriage, so by the time the paperwork makes a divorce final, you're at acceptance. If you've dated only a short amount of time you may be attached to the potential of the relationship. Since potential is something that's yet to be realized, it may be harder to fully see where the relationship didn't work than when you've been *living* what didn't work for an extended period of time. Of course, the person who thought they were married to their ideal mate and then loses them may be devastated.

It all depends on the people involved and the experiences in the relationship. Remember, you and your experiences are unique. Take the time necessary to grieve and let go of relationships that haven't worked for you. Going through the grief process is a different experience for everyone. It can take a few days, weeks, or months to go through the stages, depending on the person and circumstances surrounding the ending of a relationship. Just be aware of where you are and where you are trying to go.

Stages of Grief

As you go through life's dark tunnels, there is always light at both ends.
ANONYMOUS

The five stages of grief are denial, bargaining, anger, depression, and acceptance.

Denial is your refusal to believe that the relationship isn't working out. You may spend a lot of time justifying why, at the moment, the person you believed to be your ideal mate isn't calling you, is acting aloof, or is being just plain rude. Since you may be getting mixed signals from them about the importance of the relationship, you cling to the one positive sign and ignore and justify all of the rest, which aren't positive. For example, they may call you one night and say they've been busy at work and that they'll call you in a couple of days. A month ago they would've kept their verbal commitment. But a week goes by and you still haven't heard from them. Maybe ten days later they call and again act aloof, but you hang on to the fact they're stressed at work.

The next thing you'll do is start *bargaining* with yourself and maybe even with God. You're hoping and praying to God, asking for this one favor. If God would just help create a divine intervention to show your ideal mate what a wonderful person you are and why they should worship the ground you walk on, you'll never ask for anything ever again. You may bargain to lose weight, quit expecting your ideal mate to do what they commit to because expectations aren't spiritual, or ignore things that are on your needs list of ideal mate characteristics. Bargaining, in the grief process, isn't about negotiating and finding a mutually agreeable solution to problems. It's about when you are ignoring healthy boundaries that help you value yourself as a person and the things you need and want in a relationship.

Eventually we get *angry* that our potential ideal mate is a jerk, has rejected us, or hasn't returned our feelings. Don't disregard or ignore your anger. Since anger isn't a comfortable feeling, we may be tempted to try to put a lid on it, stick it on a shelf in the closet, turn out the light, close the door, and lock it. Often people who are actively trying to live a spiritual life may feel they don't have a right to be angry because it's not a spiritual feeling. The only problem with this is that eventually the box you locked in your emotional suitcase will be found. It may be during your next relationship or the one after that, but eventually it'll be found, dusted off, and opened up. Anger is a normal human emotion. When anger is appropriately used it's a good thing because it can motivate us to make changes. We should use the energy anger gives us to move forward. If we aren't aware of our feelings, we can get stuck in anger. When we're stuck in anger we project it at any person that may be a prospective ideal mate. This is the beginning of self-sabotaging relationships. Alternatively, we may just want to get even with whoever hurt us. If you believe in karma, or reaping what you sow, don't waste your energy on getting even. God is a better judge and jury than any human being can ever be. Eventually, if you want to avoid repeating the same themes that continue to hurt you, you'll have to forgive your offenders. Forgiveness happens in its own time, so don't expect it to happen overnight. But you must first allow yourself to feel the anger and work through it. Use it to make changes that will positively affect your life and future relationships.

As the grieving process moves forward, you'll end up *depressed*. This is a state that most of us want to avoid at all costs—even to the extent of medicating ourselves with alcohol, drugs, food, sex, gambling, and multiple other addictions that create a false sense of feeling high. When you're depressed you'll be sad and blue and cry over the possibilities of what the relationship was or could have been. You may feel that you'll never meet anyone else you would want to date. A state of hopelessness can develop. But the good news is, this too shall pass. You can't deny your feelings, including depression, but you need to do things to help you move through them. Science has proven that exercise can help lessen the physical (chemical) reaction of depression. If you're going to a gym, think of the new friends you may make. Also, there are certain comfort foods that can help lessen depression—chocolate, red wine, and cheese—because they trigger beneficial brain chemicals. (Of course, you'll want to do these things in moderation.) Make sure you go out and do things that make you happy. Visit with friends, find a new hobby, or learn a new language. You may be inclined to stay home, mope, and cry. It's all right to indulge your need to hibernate and let your wounds heal. Just don't become a recluse. In time your moments of depression will lessen.

Finally, one day you'll wake up and have found *acceptance*. This is when you may be thanking God for those unanswered prayers. You'll be able to look back at the relationship and be grateful for the things you learned. You may even be able to laugh about some of the ironic experiences in the relationship. Although acceptance is always the goal, it's something that you can't force to happen. By allowing yourself to experience your feelings when you feel them, you'll get to acceptance faster.

You may even backslide occasionally and go through brief moments of denial, bargaining, anger, and depression. The moments should be fewer and last for less time, but recognize that they are part of the process.

Each and every relationship we participate in, regardless of how much time we're in it, is an opportunity for us to learn about ourselves. It's an opportunity to allow our soul to open up, expand, and grow.

I participated in many relationships before I met my ideal mate. I know that letting someone go whom you feel a connection to can be a painful experience. But anytime I had to let a relationship go that wasn't working out, I always trusted the spiritual process. I believed all things happen as they are meant to. Every experience, including having to let someone go, was ultimately in my highest good and a part of God's plan for my life. Every past relationship took me one person closer to my ideal mate.

Anytime you are able to be in an effortless state of love, even if it's for a short amount of time, there's a success in the relationship.

Spiritual Growth

*You are free to choose, but the choices you make today will determine what
you will have, be and do in the tomorrow of your life.*
ZIG ZIGLER

All relationships are opportunities for our soul to grow. As I discussed in "Law of Preparation and Attraction," the people who cross your path are a mirror to a part of your soul. Sometimes we like the mirror. For example, you meet a loving, nice, and outgoing friend. You may even be surprised about how much you have in common. You're kindred spirits and are instantly friends for life. Of course, this same rule applies also to traits that we mirror and that we would prefer to sweep under the carpet, like anger, fear, or indecision. But in accordance with universal law, we will attract people into our lives to help us work through these issues.

All relationships are therefore stepping-stones that allow us to eventually find our ideal mate. They teach us lessons and prepare us to meet our ideal mate. Some people just seem to have more stepping-stone relationships than others. Each soul enters the earthly plane with its own relationship karma.

In some ways relationships are like grades in school. You go to preschool, kindergarten, elementary, middle school, high school, and in some cases trade school or college. Rarely does a six-year-old skip elementary school and advance into middle school. On occasion there is a young genius among us, but they're the exception and not the rule.

My point is that when you are having to let go of a relationship, realize that the experience was a necessary part of your learning experience, just like completing the fifth grade was necessary before you could go to the sixth grade. You may not have liked your fifth-grade teacher or the homework assignments, but when you began the sixth grade you were grateful for the lessons that prepared you for your new assignments. You may have even been grateful for the mean fifth-grade teacher. The same rule applies in relationships: your last one and the ones before helped prepare you for the next one. Eventually you'll get your diploma or ideal mate for a lifetime if that's what you want.

That's why it's equally important to leave, or let go of, the relationship in a state of love. If you're angry, resentful, hostile, looking to get even, or basically living in a state of fear over your last relationship or relationships, then what type of ideal mate will you be attracting?

In some cases you may believe that your partner was completely in the wrong or it was all their fault. They did you wrong, and you were an innocent victim. If this is the case, then you still must let the relationship go in love and believe in the universal Law of Cause and Effect. The Universe has its own justice system, a higher law with tougher penalties than you could ever impose. A mentor of mine once said, "The wheels of karma grind slow, but are just." Basically you need to stay out of the getting-even business and let the Universe take care of it. Taking care of yourself and your life is your business.

When you stay in a state of fear, it takes a tremendous amount of energy from you and your life. You spend time feeling angry, sad, and suspicious, projecting your feelings onto other potential mates, constantly thinking about what they are doing, and feeling sorry for yourself because you have felt rejected. This is all energy that you could and should be applying to making yourself the ideal mate you want to attract. There isn't one person on the planet who can't improve their body, mind, and soul. Remember, you attract what you project.

Imagine yourself at a dance. Every dance represents different lessons you are learning this lifetime. Lessons include working through fear, anger, and insecurities, but they also include joy, laughing, and the most important lesson of all: love. Now, at this dance they play music for many different kinds of dances—two-stepping, waltzes, tangos, jitterbug, and cheek-to-cheek slow dancing. A dance begins and you may start with one partner, but someone else may cut in during the dance. When the song changes, your partner may or may not change. You move from one partner to the next depending on when you need a different teacher to learn different lessons. Some partners may want to learn only the tango with you. When the tango ends they may decide to go to their next partner and tango again. It just depends on how much they want to tango. Others may start with the tango but also are interested in learning a waltz and anything else the band plays. They may be more interested in dancing with *you* than in what the dance is. Think of your past relationships as dances where you learned about yourself and what you are looking for in a lifetime dancing partner.

We attract people who are mirrors of the lessons we need to learn. Let's say that during a relationship you recognize you have a fear of intimacy and work through your fear instead of acting out inappropriately. By that I mean that in the past when you felt someone was getting too close to you emotionally, you'd start pushing them away and finding fault with all of their actions; eventually the relationship would end. But this time you admitted your fears and made choices that were healthy for you and the relationship. However, if one of your partner's mirrors in the relationship is also a fear of intimacy and they aren't ready to work through that fear during your relationship, eventually you won't be mirroring the same soul growth opportunity. Once one person learns a lesson that the relationship was mirroring, either the other person will have to begin reflecting the same changes or the friction will increase. It's as if one partner is trying to do the tango while the other is doing a waltz. Your rhythm is off, your feet get tangled, and you're not sure who's leading. At least when you're trying to do the same dance, there's a good chance, even though you may occasionally miss a beat, that you'll flow with the music. This is the soul growth opportunity that every relationship potentially offers.

Sometimes the relationship lessons aren't always huge soul-searching karmic experiences. The lessons may be as simple as what we want or don't want in a relationship. It may take several relationships for you to have a clear understanding of lifestyle compatibility.

You may have thought and dreamed that a professional musician was your ideal mate. An opportunity was created by the Universe for you to meet. You did, and you dated. However, at some point you realized that the constant touring and erratic hours weren't compatible with your ideal life. Since the relationship gave you firsthand experience so you could find out for yourself that the lifestyle didn't meet your needs, it certainly wasn't a waste of time, energy, or love.

You may also date someone who's funny and witty, knows how a phone works, and uses it. They make you feel special. Unfortunately, there isn't that soul-connecting chemistry that you need in a relationship. Since you can't create it, you eventually break up. But was the relationship a waste of time? No. It taught you that people actually exist who have traits that are on your ideal mate list. Maybe you even had some fun and soul-healing laughs.

Remember, every relationship can teach you something about yourself and how to live in love, even if it was only for brief moments. When you understand the positive things that a relationship taught you, it's easier to let it go in love.

After college, Melanie worked for about two years before her company transferred her to another state. She was young, excited, and completely immersed in her career. Marriage wasn't a priority for her. Her parents had had a bad marriage and divorced when she was a teenager. Melanie and her younger brother chose to live with her father, and Melanie found herself in the role of substitute mother for her brother, helping to run the household. Now, a few years later, in her first experience on her own, she wasn't eager to plan a return to the role of caretaker by becoming a wife and mother anytime in the near future.

She seemed to attract men who wanted only to sleep with her. She didn't make time for them, because she was working all of the time. She certainly didn't want any man thinking he could control any part of her life.

About a month after she settled into her new job, she started feeling lonely. She didn't know anyone except the people in her office. She started trying to make friends. She met her next-door neighbor, Rusty. They quickly be-

came friends. She recognized almost instantly that they were kindred spirits. She'd never felt that way about any man in her life.

Their friendship quickly grew, yet their relationship did not progress smoothly. Melanie felt for the first time in her life that she might like to have a permanent relationship with a man. Rusty would talk to her, he was affectionate without trying to "jump her bones," and they enjoyed the same things, like movies, theater, and volunteer work.

Despite the wonderful things in the relationship, Rusty seemed to send mixed signals about the type of relationship he wanted. Melanie would become temperamental in verbalizing her frustrations to Rusty about his mixed signals. It was as if every time they would get close, someone would start a fight.

This relationship became an emotionally grueling four-year journey for both Melanie and Rusty. They brought out each other's best and worst traits. When things were going well, life seemed heavenly, but when things were going bad, it was hell.

One night Melanie had a dream about herself and Rusty. On a gray, cloudy day they were at a train station. Melanie was hugging Rusty good-bye. Although he didn't have any luggage, she was aware that he might be gone for quite some time. She heard a voice bellowing from the sky, "Let him go. If he returns he'll be yours forever."

Once Melanie woke up she knew that they needed to end the relationship because it wasn't good for either of them. Letting go of Rusty was the most difficult thing she ever had to do.

She realized that Rusty came into her life to show her that she actually could trust a man and that she wanted one day to have a husband and family. Rusty taught her about love. He'd been a safe person for her to learn from about what she wanted in a mate.

It took her a long time to get over Rusty because he never came back. But she does feel blessed; because of her relationship with Rusty, she knows what works and doesn't work for her.

Karen had been married for ten years to a man who she thought was her soulmate. They were each independent people, but in the course of ten years *their personal and professional lives had become very intertwined. During their time together they had explored many things in the New Age spiritual movement. For example, if they wanted to create something they would make goal lists, meditate, and visualize it together. More often than not they were able to create the business opportunity, personal growth experience, or material item they were seeking.*

One day Karen's husband got involved in a spiritual movement that she was uncomfortable with. Eventually, he told her she had to join him in this experience or they would have to break up. She didn't believe he would leave her for what she termed a cult, but he did. She went through an emotionally draining divorce. She was left with their house and a huge mortgage. He'd taken all of the businesses they had built together, which left her financially strapped.

Karen had believed her husband was her soulmate and part of her life force. If he wasn't part of her life, she thought, she would literally die. She became physically ill and emotionally unstable.

Her mother insisted that she come home to Virginia for Thanksgiving. On her way home, at the airport between flights, a man called Karen's name and walked toward her. Being in a fragile emotional state, she became fearful and started running. When he finally caught up with her she realized it was Greg, an old high-school friend.

They exchanged phone numbers, and Greg said he'd love to visit. He called that week and said he could come the following weekend. Karen said, "Oh, yeah, that'll be great." Then she freaked out, called her friends, and told them they had to come over and spend the weekend with her. She wasn't quite ready to be alone with a man. Although she trusted Greg and she'd been dating, she wasn't looking to get serious. Greg came over, and they all had a nice weekend.

That Christmas, Greg surprised Karen with an unexpected gift, a watch. At that point, she realized he cared for her, and she began to think about allowing herself to enter into a romantic relationship with him.

After about three months they finally began dating. Greg helped Karen become focused on getting a new job and moving away from where she lived. He felt she needed to move from her house, which had so many memories of her marriage, and begin a new life. He even offered to share his one-room apartment while she was getting resettled.

Within a month, she found a new job and moved into Greg's tiny apartment. The next few months were stressful while Karen was waiting to sell her house. Greg's place was cramped, and eventually it caused stress on the relationship. They realized they just weren't compatible as a couple.

Five months later, after her house sold, Karen moved out of Greg's and into her own place. Her relationship with Greg had deteriorated severely by that point. Karen had deep feelings for Greg because she felt he had rescued her from a horrible place in her life. Eventually the relationship and even their friendship fizzled.

However, Karen is grateful to Greg for walking into her life at a time she needed support and for giving her a shoulder to lean on. It just shows that all relationships serve their purpose, even if they aren't meant to last a lifetime.

Why People Hang On to Relationships That Aren't Working

Follow the first law of holes: if you are in one, stop digging.
DENNIS HEALEY

When we're trying to actually live a spiritual life, we tend to place emphasis on the positive. Letting go of something that we thought we wanted isn't viewed as a rite of passage in our culture. To the contrary, it's usually viewed as a failure because we're taught to respect acquisitions, control, and power. Letting go, by definition, doesn't include any of these things. Ultimately, we tend to cling to relationships and things because of our perception that letting go isn't actually growth or in our best interest. It may require us to feel some emotional pain, which we want to avoid at all cost. It actually feels safer hanging on to something that's familiar even though it's uncomfortable. So we attach to hope, fear, and ego in an attempt to keep the familiar feelings around us.

Hope

I believe the biggest reason people hang on to relationships that aren't working is *hope*. From the time we are children we are read the stories of Cinderella, Snow White, and Sleeping Beauty. The common thread is that the prince rescues the damsel in distress and they get married and live happily ever after. The only problem is, the stories forget to tell us *how* to live happily ever after. The implication is, all we have to do is know who our prince or princess is and everything else falls into place.

When we quit reading fairy tales we progress to TV and movie fairy tales. Again, heroes and heroines fall in love, and despite all obstacles, the ending is an implied happily-ever-after. Even in *Gone With the Wind*, Scarlett quits crying on the steps of her grand mansion and says, "Tomorrow is another day." The implication is that everything will probably work out. When movies or books mimic life, like *The Bridges of Madison County*, we call them romantic tragedies. But we bond to the romantic tragedy because we can cry, hope, and wish for the fairy-tale ending that we're looking for in our own life.

In addition to the fairy tales that taught us about living happily ever after, we live in a country that was *built on hope*. From the Pilgrims who landed at Plymouth Rock to the immigrants who went through Ellis Island to the numbers of people who are willing to risk their lives by crossing oceans and rivers to enter the borders of America today, each and every one has one thing in common—*hope* for a better life. The greatest thing about America is the opportunity for success. This means the commercialization of *hope*. Hope is the foundation for selling most products, services, and businesses. If you just invest in this or that moneymaking program, you can get rich. If you wear this makeup and that designer label and work out at this gym, you'll look beautiful. If you attend this workshop or seminar, you'll find inner peace. Now, don't misunderstand. In some cases the hope that's being sold can help you manifest the desired results, but it also takes effort on your part. Just owning a StairMaster will not help you lose weight. You actually have to get on it, turn it on, and sweat. It takes the selling of a hope *and* your efforts to get the desired results. Wishful thinking alone isn't enough.

Anyone who's pursuing life on a spiritual path is told to be kind and loving and not to expect anything. With these characteristics, if we're in a struggling relationship, all we have to hang on to is the *hope* that if we love someone enough, things will work out. It's necessary to be kind and loving. But we do have to expect that we will be happy. If the relationship we're in isn't making us happy, that may be an unanswered prayer. Your ideal mate may be around the next corner.

Hope in relationships is often based on people changing. Circumstances may change and miracles can happen—but if a person's basic character trait is being aloof or a workaholic, for example, in most cases these are the kinds of things that won't change, barring a spiritual awakening. Unfortunately, people on Earth aren't in a position to create a spiritual awakening for someone else. If a person's character traits aren't on your list of ideal mate traits, then it's time to move on. That person in most cases will never be able to be the person you are looking for. It will always be as if you went shopping for a red dress, couldn't find one that you liked, and settled for a pink one. You hang it in your closet *hoping* it will turn red.

Now, everyone knows stories of people who gave the person they believed with all their heart and soul was their ideal mate time to work through all of their own fears and obstacles. One might say that such people were clinging to *hope*. But I argue that they intuitively had faith that the relationship would work. Yes, they may have had to let go of the relationship for a period of time, in some cases a long period, but in the end they had faith that everything would work out.

How do you know the difference between hope and faith?

Hope is a *desire* and *wish* that something is true. You intuitively don't feel that everything is all right, so you have to logically justify situations to yourself, friends, and others. You analyze every aspect of the situation and look for facts that help you justify your theories and conclusions. If others disagree with your hope ideas, you become defensive and angry and may even look for additional facts to help substantiate your hope. Hope includes denial. Remember the first phase of the grieving process. For example, your boyfriend, whom you've been dating for three years, will not marry you. He says he doesn't want to make a commitment. Your intuition led you to believe that he was cheating on you. You followed your instincts and discovered you were right. This happened several times during the relationship. But you continued to believe that in time he would settle down and want to make a commitment to you. The facts revealed—and your intuition knew—that something in the relationship wasn't the way it was supposed to be, but you chose to ignore it in the hope that he would change. Your chances that someone will change based on someone else's hopes are worse than your chances of winning the lottery. There's always a *possibility*, but in some cases you need to factor in *probability*.

Faith is when you simply *know* something to be true. You often hear people say that for as long as they could remember, they knew they would be a doctor, writer, or musician. Some would say this is destiny. Faith and destiny may very well be linked, but the point is that faith is knowing something will happen before it's manifested. You don't even have to question it. That doesn't mean you don't have to work for it, but the inner knowing is just there. You may not have evidence or any logic to substantiate your faith, but it's not about proof. Faith isn't fearful or anxious. In your reality, whatever you have faith in is a definite done deal. You have a confidence that it's already happened; it's just a question of when. Faith is the little voice you feel and can occasionally hear, when you begin to have doubts about a situation, that regardless of how dark the storm clouds seem to be, you will find the rainbow after the storm. When you have faith you have an inner knowing that despite the obvious, everything will work out. You don't need to justify or explain the situation to yourself, family, or friends. It's a belief that extends to the core of your soul. Even if you have faith, you may question it from time to time, but in the end you're able to be at that special place where you're one with God. You may find this peaceful connection when you meditate, pray, or go to the beach. When I agreed to write this book about attracting your ideal mate, I wondered if I was the best person for the job, because at the time I had not met my lifelong ideal mate. But I had faith in the process and knew that I would meet him. By the time the contracts for the book were finalized, I had met Jim.

Fear

The second reason we cling to relationships that aren't working is *fear*. If you're single, our culture tells you that something is wrong with this status. You aren't part of the group with the mate, house, and 2.5 children. Since we like to fit in and be a part of a group, this only alienates us and enhances the fear that we won't find our ideal mate. Then, when we meet someone, we have a tendency to feel we have to make the relationship work out. We feel we need to find Mr. or Miss Ideal Mate despite the fact that we may still be defining exactly what it is we want in a mate, not to mention becoming the ideal mate to match the one we're looking for.

Eventually you may reach an age when you are afraid to be alone. Fortunately, times have changed and people are marrying later in life. But if you decide that you're going to make a relationship work out just because you don't want to be alone, remember that the loneliest place in the world is in a room in which you're with the wrong person. If your partner doesn't meet your needs, you'll be struggling to fill the void. Eventually, you'll just be angry because the person you think should fill the void can't, and you'll start blaming them for the failure of the relationship. Deep down you'll then become angry with yourself because you knew this person didn't have the traits and characteristics that fit you. You're continuing the vicious cycle of settling for what you don't want and what doesn't work for you. A person can't make you feel less lonely because they're a warm body lying next to you at night. In fact, if there isn't a holistic connection that pulls at your heart and soul, then the relationship will eventually begin to drain you. It will be a life-sucking instead of life-giving force. This creates more emotional and spiritual emptiness that needs to be filled and certainly isn't worth the extra energy just to avoid physical loneliness. Instead, use the energy to do things that will fill you up emotionally and spiritually. As you become the person who is your ideal mate, it will enable you to attract your ideal mate.

You may just be tired of choosing Mr. or Miss Wrongs. You don't want to have to tell the world that this relationship didn't work out—again. You may want to cling to something that you feel isn't or wasn't right for you in the first place just because it's easier. You may get tired of people asking to set you up on blind dates or feeling sorry for you because you're alone on the holidays. But trust me, if the relationship didn't work out it's better to deal with the empathy from your friends and family than to try to fit a square peg into a round hole. *Each and every relationship you're in is an ideal mate for that moment in time.* You're in each

other's lives to be a catalyst for growth. All relationships help you grow
as a person, and eventually you'll meet your lifelong ideal mate.

If you're holding on to a relationship out of fear, then you need to
identify the exact causes of the fear. If you understand what the fear is,
you will then be able to work through it. You can't work through something that you don't understand. If you don't understand and work
through your fear, you're at risk for repeating the same type of relationships over and over again.

Ego

Often our egos get attached to who was right or wrong in a relationship. This can be about issues or about the relationship itself. When we
are attached to right and wrong it's difficult to let go and move forward.
We live in a culture that preaches that being right is the most important
thing on earth. However, from a spiritual perspective the most important thing is love. This includes not only loving others, but also loving
yourself. Michael Ryce, who teaches workshops about relationships,
states that if you have a choice between being right and choosing love,
always choose love. Sometimes choosing to live in love means walking
away and letting the relationship go. It may be better for you and the
other person.

Have you ever known someone who loved plants but had a reputa-
tion for killing them? Maybe they watered them too much or forgot to
water them. Perhaps they never let them get sunlight or left them outside during the winter. Or maybe they just didn't have a green thumb despite following all the directions about growing plants to a tee. Finally
one day they acquire a new plant and decide this one will not die under
any circumstances. It gets sick. They put all of their time and energy
into trying to save the plant. It dies anyway because it had an incurable
fungus at the root. In the process of trying to save this one plant because
they wanted everyone to quit calling them Lethal Green Thumbs, their
other plants also got sick and eventually died. If you're focusing all of
your time and energy into trying to save something that cannot be saved,
then you may be missing opportunities to grow other things.

Living in a state of love and detaching from your ego in relationships isn't about letting people walk all over you. On the contrary, everyone should have healthy boundaries. Knowing what you want and expect in a relationship will help you develop healthy boundaries. If someone repeatedly crosses them inappropriately, then you should move forward. It's better to move on and leave a negative situation than stick around because you want to be right. In the end it won't matter. The satisfaction of being right is a short-lived feeling compared to the frustrations you go through trying to be right.

When you're in a relationship that doesn't work out, it's easy to hang on to the hope, fear, and ego-based beliefs that stop you from moving forward and growing. I like to think of each relationship as a step on a staircase. When you get to the top you've met your life mate. Some staircases are small, only a few steps, and others have what seems like hundreds of stairs. But if you want to get to the top, you have to take each step, one at a time. If you try to skip steps you risk falling down. Don't forget that in some buildings you may reach what you perceive is the top of the staircase, only to find another set of stairs waiting to take you higher.

Was It Love, or Fear?

Love is a space in which all other emotions can be experienced.
ROBERT PRINABLE

Fear is not the present but only past and future.
A COURSE IN MIRACLES

Love is about wanting what's best not only for yourself, but for the ones you love as well. Love isn't selfish. Sometimes love is about letting go and moving forward. If, after you've gone through some of the grieving process, you're still having a hard time moving into forgiveness and letting go, ask yourself the following questions:

- If I really love myself, why would I want to be with someone who doesn't reciprocate the feeling?
- If I love the other person, do I want them to do whatever they feel is necessary to grow and be happy, even if that means not being with me?

I know sometimes it's easier to wallow in the "poor me," victim syndrome about relationships that don't work out as we hoped. But if you really love yourself and your last partner, you'll eventually move into wanting what's best for both of you. I assure you that if you're not together, there's a reason for it. Despite the wisdom any of us can gain on Earth, we will never know more than God.

If you can't eventually look back on the relationship with a feeling of love and gratitude for having experienced it, then ask yourself, "What was its foundation? Was it built on feelings of love, or fear?" If the relationship was built on true love, then even when you hurt you'll only want good things for the other person. If it was built on fear, your interest will be in controlling and possessing the other person. You'll believe *your* "how to live life" guide is the one they need to follow, despite their need to become an individual person. Understanding your patterns in past relationships can help you identify why you're in relationships based on fear and will help you quit attracting them, or at least to say, "No, thank you," when they show up at your relationship door.

Trust me. By taking the high road you'll eventually reap back your goodwill. It's the law of the Universe. You get what you put out.

Patterns in Past Relationships

You keep on getting what you've been getting, when you
keep doing what you've been doing.
ANONYMOUS

Part of making the letting-go experience easier is understanding why you were in the relationship in the first place. In her book *It's All in the Playing,* Shirley MacLaine explains that every person has a theme that's unique to their life. Some people are in dramas, others are in comedies, romances, tragedies, or action adventures. For instance, if your theme is drama, even when you change leading actors, sets, support cast members, and scripts, your theme remains a drama. For instance, *Casablanca* and *Alien* have very different scripts, but they are both dramas.

If you're tired of the theme that you keep repeating in your life, the only way to move past it is to understand it and make changes. You may never be able to escape your karmic life theme, but you can pick better scripts that are more appealing to you. In order to really understand why you keep attracting the same type of person, you'll have to do some inner work to understand your past and the mirror it's creating for you. I believe the easiest and quickest way to become aware of your sabotaging mirrors was developed by Dr. Barbara DeAngelis. She describes the activities in detail in *Are You the One for Me?* I'll highlight some of them here.

The first thing you do is write an "emotional want ad" for the kind of mate you would like to attract. Most people would write an ad similar to this:

> *WANTED: Attractive, loving, sensitive person for a mutually fulfilling lifelong partnership. Must be able to share feelings, be unafraid of intimacy, and physically/emotionally available. Must adore the ground I walk on. Must be successful, but not work too much. If you're emotionally healthy, faithful, honest, and looking to make a lifelong commitment, call me.*

The next ad you need to write is for the type of person you've actually been attracting into your life. This ad might sound more like this:

> *WANTED: Are you unable to make a commitment? Not aware of your feelings? Unable to communicate? I'm looking for someone to share a long, painful, noncommitted, noncommunicative, mixed-signal, and sexually frustrating relationship. I'll give you an itemized list of your character defects, what created them, and how you can transcend them. Little time or energy is required on your part. I'd rather analyze why you're ignoring me or being mean to me than actually spend time with you. But call anytime, even after you've spent an unannounced extended period of time in your cave. If you like being evasive, believe the best philosophy in life is "Sins of omission are better than sins of commission," and don't know how to use a phone, then call me.*

Now, this may seem extreme, but it'll give you a chance to be honest about the mates you've been ordering from the Universe. It may even help you laugh about the extreme dysfunction of the relationships you keep allowing in your life. If you want to change the type of person you keep attracting in your life, then you'll have to write a different want ad.

To help you understand why you've been attracting and accepting the person who answers the second ad you've been writing, you need to make a list of every partner you've had a *significant* relationship with. These aren't people you dated only a few times. It may even be just one person if that's the only partner you've had. Then, list all of their negative qualities—personality traits you dislike the most—in a word or two. For example your list might include *angry, dishonest, moody, jobless, self-absorbed,* or *lying.* Don't list positive traits. Once you've completed the list for each partner, circle any words that repeat themselves. Make a summary list of those words or qualities that were repeated. Do you notice any trends? Do some of the same traits and qualities keep showing up over and over again?

The next step is to begin to understand your emotional programming. "Emotional programming is a set of decisions and beliefs you made about yourself, others and the world when you were growing up," states Dr. DeAngelis. According to psychologists, you received most of this programming by the time you were five.

You need to make a list of the most painful situations and events that happened to you in your childhood. Your list might include things like *My parents were divorced* or *Dad never came to my birthday parties* or *Mom was an alcoholic.* After each thing on the list, write down a decision you made about how you felt about yourself. If your dad didn't come to your birthday party, you may have decided that men are irresponsible—and not to count on them. Eventually that may have led to relationships with men who are irresponsible and whom you can't count on. After all, that's the message you got in your childhood.

We often re-create the emotional home environment we grew up in, not because we liked it but because it feels comfortable, because its games are those we already know how to play. If in your mind you believed your home was supposed to equal love but your home was lonely, then you may believe love and loneliness are the same thing. If you haven't learned what your subconscious mirror is, then it's impossible to change it.

The next step is to make a complaint list for each of your parents. Compare it to the negative trait list from your significant relationships. Are there any overlapping traits? Are you dating people who have the same negative characteristics as one or both of your parents? Are you consciously or subconsciously trying to fix a situation from your childhood?

These exercises may take some time. You may have to discuss them with some of your friends to get a completely honest inventory. I encourage you to read and do the exercises in chapter two, "Why We Choose the People We Love," in *Are You the One for Me?* It'll give you full and complete examples and explanations.

Only by increasing your awareness of your emotional patterns can you begin to change them. But the good news is, you can change them. It takes work and effort on your part, but it'll be well worth the effort. If you are feeling overwhelmed by your pattern list, you may want to consider professional counseling or support groups to help you understand and accept your past so you can let go and move forward.

Julie's friend Joanna had a college degree, was taking graduate courses, and was politically active. She was a great organizer and administrator. However, she kept going from one secretarial job to another. She told Julie, about three years after college, "I don't want to be a secretary anymore."

"Well, Joanna, there's one way not to get a secretarial job next time," Julie said.

Joanna got all excited and eagerly said, "How, how? Tell me!"

"Don't apply for one," Julie responded.

It was that simple. Joanna never applied for another secretarial job and now has a highly placed administrative position.

Julie thinks people end up in situations because it's the role they apply for, whether consciously or subconsciously. If you don't want to end up with a mate with traits you don't like, then don't apply to be the mate of such a person. If you wonder why you keep attracting a certain kind of person, you're probably looking for traits or a lifestyle that comes with that type of person. You may also be playing a role that forces the other person to play a role mirroring you.

It occurred to Julie that she'd been in a relationship with a man who played the role of her father. Although there were many very good parts to the relationship and the man, unlike Julie's father, was supportive of her both personally and professionally, he still played a fatherlike role while Julie played a daughterlike role.

This relationship had soulmate energy and a bond of spirit unlike any other Julie had ever experienced. Even after it was over, it took a couple of years for her to realize that if she didn't want a relationship where someone was playing father to her, she'd have to make sure she didn't play daughter.

Julie wasn't consciously aware that she was acting like a daughter, because she's a very independent person. Julie isn't a needy woman; she wasn't looking for someone to take care of her financially or in any other way. Yet she realized that the first relationship every girl has with a man is the one she has with her father. That's where she learns how to relate to men and what role to play.

Julie realized she was acting like a daughter and that she'd been attracting father types in her romantic relationships. She kept looking to "perform for Daddy" and to seek approval by saying, "Look at me, look at what I did." For example, in her work, she couldn't wait to show her boyfriend her projects, but not in the way she'd show them to other colleagues. Because he and she were in the same field he could relate to what she did and why she did it. But she'd present it to him like the eager little girl who was delighted that she was going to be clever for Daddy.

"I was like a Shirley Temple who was a precocious four-year-old going on forty, smiling with a big grin, saying, 'Look what I did,'" Julie said. "Of course, I didn't act that way, but it was how I was feeling inside. I'm sure some of that energy was surrounding my actions.

"Then my boyfriend would play his part and get all excited just like a proud daddy," Julie said.

Finally she realized it was like a diet. If you need to change the way you eat and you know you have a real weakness for potatoes of all kinds—french fries, mashed potatoes, baked potatoes, and potato chips—you can't break your potato addiction by deciding that you'll eat all kinds of potatoes except potato chips, or that you'll eat only french fries. You have to give up every kind of potato. Eventually, you may gradually be able to add potatoes back into your diet in a healthy way.

Julie felt relationships are like that. If you have a pattern that isn't healthy for you, you'll have to break it cold turkey. You'll have to completely eliminate anything that may seem to resemble it from your relationships, even if the pattern isn't inherently harmful, until you can grasp the reason you established the pattern in the first place. You'll have to have an understanding of where the pattern came from, why you're doing it, how you can break it, what positive behavior can be substituted for the old one, what could be a new way to think of it, and how to change your response to buttons that get pushed and start the pattern. Once you clear out all of the old baggage, you can then reintroduce some of the healthier aspects of that old pattern.

So, in her next relationship Julie didn't apply for the role of daughter and found a partner instead of a father.

When Sherry looked back on her relationships, she realized that they all had common themes: looking for love, being rescued and completed. She also realized she never selected any of the men she was involved with; she was chosen by them, and this made it very difficult to let go when the relationships didn't work out.

When she met Jerry, she was seventeen and he was twenty-two. She was finishing high school and was heading to college, and he was finishing college and going to veterinary school. They dated and wrote to each other for three years before they married. Sherry was head over heels in love with Jerry. She was also hoping to be rescued from a physically and verbally abusive mother.

Even though she thought she was a complete person, she felt she wanted to be rounded out. "Thinking someone else can complete you sounds fine and good, but until you're in the day-to-day functioning of the relationship, you don't realize you have to be a complete person yourself before you can be in a healthy relationship," Sherry said. "You need another person to share in your completeness, not to complete you. If you're not already complete, it becomes a competition about who's going to be completed."

After fifteen years of a loveless, cold relationship with someone who'd been diagnosed as a psychopath, she decided she had to leave Jerry when she saw their two children mimicking his emotionally cold behaviors. Originally she believed that she should stay married for the sake of the children, but when she recognized it was hurting them, she knew she wasn't giving them the loving home she wanted to. When she left, the divorce was amicable. However,

Jerry eventually decided he wanted to have custody of the two children and to see Sherry's life fall apart.

She spent the next six years in custody fights, having her home broken into and trying to survive. On many occasions she'd walk into her home and realize someone had broken into her filing cabinet. Initially she'd want to retaliate. When she had these thoughts, Jerry's negative actions would continue. Sherry felt the Universe was telling her she had to let go of Jerry in love and bless him. When she wanted to get even she was only adding fuel to the negative energy.

One day she was in a serious car accident because the master brake cylinder of her car had been damaged. After the accident she sent a mechanic to the wrecking yard to check the car and try to determine if there were any other causes for the accident. The master brake cylinder had been stolen while the car was locked up in the wrecking yard. She felt this was a sign that Jerry would stop at nothing, and she had to forgive, bless, and let him go so she could continue with her life. Once she started blessing Jerry and visualizing him in loving white light, the retaliations stopped.

Through the years she has had several other relationships with men she felt she connected with on a soul level. Again, they all picked her, but she recognized the spiritual connection. The relationships were all abusive in some way: verbally, emotionally, or even physically. All of these men were, like her, professional and well educated.

During times of abuse or stalking she'd ask for assistance from the archangel Michael and his host of angels. Miraculously, many times the abuser or stalker would leave.

She learned to increase her boundaries in each subsequent relationship, although she still never chose whom she became involved with. When you feel powerless, letting go is hard because your feelings of rejection, anger, and hurt overcome your spiritual nature.

In one of her relationships, the man proposed one morning. That night when she stopped by his house she found him in bed with an ex-girlfriend. That was a turning point because Sherry realized this wasn't about her. It was his issue. "If he could propose to me that morning and make love to someone else that night, he didn't know what he wanted," Sherry said. "It also made me recognize that I didn't know what I wanted in a relationship and I was mirroring that."

Although it hurt to let go of the relationship, she was able to leave it in love. She recognized the lesson she needed to learn.

This experience helped her believe that if you leave a relationship on unhappy terms, you'll attract another one that's unhappy. Even if you have to agree to disagree, Sherry feels, it's important to leave on good terms. You can't leave a relationship projecting shame and blame about why it went wrong. If you want to attract someone who's loving and kind, you need to be in that space yourself.

Her next relationship was based on love. Sherry thinks it happened that way because she had been able to leave her previous relationship in a state of love and both she and her next mate were looking for love. Although he was much younger than she, they were very compatible and loving. Eventually the age difference created long-term compatibility problems. He wanted children, and Sherry couldn't have any more. He eventually fell in love with his running partner. The timing of the ending of this relationship wasn't good for Sherry, because of professional and personal reasons. Not that there's ever a good time to end a relationship, but this was just another stressful event among many others. She felt like a victim and was saying, "How could you do this to me?"

Sherry eventually moved out of the state for a job. Her current relationship has been stormy. The mirroring of being a victim—the way she left her last relationship—began immediately. She realizes that she'll probably need to leave this one soon.

"It's important how you end relationships," Sherry says, "because that creates the foundation for the next relationship that's coming to you."

Each time she's had to let go, she has relied on affirmations, prayer, and visualization to help her heal. She asks for divine assistance not only for herself but also for the other person.

Sherry realizes that she has to be complete and not needy before she can attract her ideal mate. She knows she doesn't have a right to ask someone to change, but she recognizes she has a right to have personal boundaries. It's about recognizing what works for you and what doesn't. It's about knowing yourself.

Sherry's working on leaving her current relationship in love. She's planning on being more active in choosing her next mate, instead of being chosen.

At forty-five, Sherry is looking forward to breaking old patterns and applying the lessons she's learned in her next relationship.

These men were ideal mates at the time Sherry attracted them because they kept bringing her lessons about personal choices and self-love. Until she learns them, these same teachers will keep appearing.

———————————————————————————————

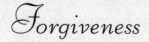

Forgiveness

To forgive is the highest most beautiful form of love. In return,
you will receive untold peace and happiness.
ROBERT MULLER

Forgiveness is an emotional state that frees us from anger, resentment, guilt, fear, and shame. As I've repeatedly said in this book, you can't—and shouldn't—deny or bury your feelings, but you should strive to move through them as quickly as possible. When you think of forgiveness, you have to remember that it includes forgiving people who have hurt you, even yourself. Forgiveness gives us an inner peace about situations that have negatively impacted our lives. Without it we'll always carry with us negative feelings and energy from situations that have caused us pain in the past.

Forgiveness is often associated with letting someone (who probably didn't follow the Golden Rule of "Do unto others as you'd have others do unto you") off the hook for their offenses. But forgiveness is ultimately about releasing *yourself* from the emotionally, mentally, and spiritually draining task of carrying with you all of the mean things other people have done to you. If you are living a life without forgiveness, pretend you are pushing a wheelbarrow, and every time someone hurts you, it becomes a rock that you throw into your wheelbarrow. You also throw rocks into your wheelbarrow every time you do something that you perceive is wrong. The rocks vary in size depending on the amount of pain each offense caused. You may have some pebbles and golf ball— and softball-sized rocks. You may even have a few boulders. Individually these rocks may not seem like a burden, but collectively they get quite heavy. Imagine collecting them for a lifetime. How many rocks are in your wheelbarrow?

Carrying anger and pain over past hurts, whether it's over something someone did to you or something you did to someone else, only serves to block your flow of energy. It causes us to separate from the universal life force called love. You forgive others to save *yourself*.

It's easy to name the rocks in our wheelbarrow that are the offenses of other people. Most of us know exactly who has hurt us and how. But what about the rocks of things you need to forgive yourself for? What about the endless string of bad relationships you've been in? Maybe you blame yourself for staying in an abusive relationship too long. But the truth is, every relationship is an opportunity for growth. It happened exactly as it should have for your soul and your spiritual growth. There is never failure in anything, only opportunity to learn and grow. Because of an experience you may have become a more empathic person. The point is, if you don't forgive yourself you're adding weight to your wheelbarrow, and that causes you to move through life more slowly.

You'll probably never have a completely empty wheelbarrow. You'll always be tested, and you will always have to forgive yourself or others for something. It's called the human experience. It's important to take a daily inventory of how many rocks you're carrying and where you are in the forgiveness process.

Forgiveness is a journey. In most cases, without divine intervention it won't happen overnight. But there are some things you can do to help speed up the process. List the exact nature of things you need to forgive yourself and others for. Now, you don't have to share these with anyone but yourself and God, if you choose. But by knowing what you are trying to forgive, you can meditate, visualize, and even ask God for help. If you understand what you are forgiving, you'll also be less likely to project those feelings of anger, blame, shame, and resentment onto others.

Forgiving yourself and others is a process that happens with time and effort. A heart that forgives allows room for love to grow. Without forgiveness your heart becomes cold and hard. Unless your ideal mate is a stone statue, forgiveness is something that you'll be practicing all of your life.

Symbols to Help You Release

Ideas by themselves cannot produce change of being; your effort must go in the right direction, and one must correspond to the other.
P. D. OUSPENSKY AND G. I. GURDJIEFF

Since the beginning of time, man has created rituals to help bridge the gap between the spiritual and physical worlds. Dances, altars, and prayers have all been used to communicate with the universal forces that are perceived as either God or the gods when people seek divine assistance. Rituals were practiced to ask for and show thanks for rain, planting the crops, hunting, marriage, and births, just to name a few occasions. Since the physical survival of earlier civilizations depended a great deal on forces beyond their control, faith in the Universe was necessary. In the past, rituals were practiced more often to connect the spiritual and physical worlds than they are today. In the modern world, if the orange crop in southern Florida is destroyed by frost, your local supermarket will get oranges from southern California. You may have to pay more, but you won't be orangeless, and you won't be threatened with starvation.

My point is that symbols and rituals are very important tools to help our logical, analytical minds create a bridge to our soul and the intangible, spiritual world. They give our mind something to grasp that represents where we are trying to be spiritually.

I've listed several techniques that may help you process and symbolize release.

- *Journaling*

    By writing what you're feeling about a relationship that you're trying to release, you process your emotions. It's a safe place to say anything you want to. You don't have to be nice, politically correct, or even right. You can say whatever you feel. Your journal should be something that's for your eyes only. If you keep your emotions inside, eventually they'll start leaking out into other areas of your life. They may show up as anger, disease, or depression, but they will eventually show up. They may even be the things that keep you from attracting your ideal mate. Journaling helps you understand your feelings and the patterns you have in relationships. You can't break patterns and habits that you don't understand. Writing down your feelings and thoughts can be the first step in letting go of things that aren't working.

- *Letters*

    It may be appropriate to write a letter to your ex or exes, sharing your feelings about the relationship. However, the fact that you write it doesn't mean that you should *mail* or *deliver* it. Writing a letter can be a form of closure. If you are inclined to mail the letter you're writing, the letter should be about your feelings about the relationship. It *shouldn't* be an attempt to get your ex to understand each and every incident in which you were inappropriately treated and how, if they could overcome their shortcomings, the two of you could live happily ever after. A letter is about closing the door and expecting nothing in return except knowing that you shared honest communication about your feelings. It should always end with gratitude about the relationship because it helped you learn and grow.

- *Prayers*

    Don't forget to ask God, or whatever you perceive as the universal force, to help you let go of people and situations that are causing you pain. The Bible says, "Ask and ye shall receive." Try it. It works.

- *Memory box*

    You may want to put all of the things that remind you of your ex in a box. The box may include pictures, letters, and gifts. This gets things that remind you of the relationship out of your daily sight. It's the "Out of sight, out of mind" principle. When you're packing your memory box, you may cry while going down memory lane. Crying is good because it releases emotions and helps us grieve. At some point you may want to throw away your memory box. But eventually you may want to put the pictures back in your photo album. So, before making any permanent decisions about its contents, make sure that you have gone through the entire grieving process. Time does heal all pain.

- *Burning bowl*

    Out of the ashes the phoenix will rise. Burning things has always symbolized endings and rebirth. If you're sure that you don't want pictures and letters, you can burn them, but I suggest that you put these things in a memory box until you are *sure* you don't want them. By this I mean making a clear, rational decision, not one out of hurt, anger, and pain. When it feels right you can burn them if appropriate. If you want to do a burning bowl ceremony early in your grieving process, write a letter or draw a picture and burn that.

- *Visualization*

    While you are meditating you can visualize the person who caused you pain in a white healing light. This may be difficult. You can visualize all of the negative feeling and energy you have toward the person who hurt you flowing through your body and exiting through your hands. You may have to practice this in short increments, but eventually you'll be able to do it with a loving feeling, and the healing will truly begin.

- *Affirmations*

    Affirmations are positive declarations of what you are expecting, not hoping, to attain. In the letting-go process, it's stating that you have forgiven and are letting the relationship go. An example is *I free myself and Todd from past hurts, hopes, and expectations of what the relationship could've been. We are free to move forward into new and more rewarding experiences.*

- *Changing your physical environment*

    You may want to rearrange your house, get new sheets, or paint a room. Anytime you change your physical environment, it changes the flow of energy. You may want to read a book about Feng Shui, the Chinese art of placement and flow. The theory is that the placement of furniture and accessories in a room make it more universally friendly to attracting what you want in your life. For example, your bedroom should have something red in it to help attract the flow of sexuality. You can also choose to clean out your closets. Either give things away or have a garage sale and get rid of old clothes, furniture, books, dishes, and other items that you aren't using but that are just taking up space. If something isn't useful and it's just collecting dust, then let it go and make room for something new.

- *Changing yourself*

    It may sound trivial, but now may be the time to get that new hairstyle, update your wardrobe, and pick up a new hobby. Change your patterns and do something different. Do things that make you feel good about yourself. Maybe it's a manicure or massage. The point is, do things that allow you to grow and become like the person you want to meet. When there is a void in your life, the best way to move through the grief is to fill the void with things that make you feel good about yourself.

- *Blowing Bubbles*

    Remember when you were a kid and you'd blow bubbles? They'd fly into the air and burst. Sometimes I like to blow bubbles and visualize my anger and hurt flying away and ultimately bursting in the air. I know this seems silly, but if it helps you laugh, it's a step toward letting go and moving forward.

There aren't any magical quick-fix solutions that take you through the letting-go experience. You can't buy, understand, or make letting go happen. It happens when you put forth the effort to understand your past, live in the present, and move toward your future. It's a unique combination for every situation that you must let go of. Patience and time are keys that allow you to feel and experience the letting-go process. Think of it as trying to cross a bridge from one island to another. In the middle of the bridge is a gate with a secret code. All of the steps you take to cross the bridge are part of the secret code that will allow you to open the gate. You may get tired and frustrated while you are trying to get the access code, but one day your efforts will pay off and the gate will open. You'll be allowed to cross the bridge into the land of letting go and forgiveness.

When I let go of what I am, I become what I might be.

JOHN HEIDER

Epilogue

The most perplexing, complicating, ecstatic, joyous, life-giving, and mysterious journey you'll ever take is the one that you take to find your ideal mate. But it won't stop there. Once you've found your ideal mate, the mysterious journey continues. You'll experience moments of sheer love and bliss that are beyond your wildest dreams. It's those very moments that will motivate you to stay in the relationship when you're going through the normal growing pains of any relationship.

From the stories I've shared, you've gotten to see that although relationships you're in may or may not work out as you either hoped or planned, they were the right relationship for you at the time you were in them. Sometimes the people whom we are in relationships with are there only to teach us a few lessons. Ultimately all relationships are here to teach us about compassion, empathy, and, most important, love.

Many people believe that finding your ideal mate is all in the hands of fate or luck—it's destiny. But I must remind you that destiny enters only when preparation meets opportunity.

Some of your temporary mates can help you prepare yourself to be in a relationship with your ideal mate, but you must do the real work internally. You must know what you're looking for in a mate and believe you deserve to find that person. You must allow your past wounds to heal and move beyond your fears of getting hurt. God doesn't want you to be hurt, and if you're hurting he'll help you through it. It's trusting and having faith that even when we hurt, we're growing and becoming wiser, more compassionate, and more loving because of the experience.

Each person who met their ideal mate was participating in the business of living. That's where all of your preparation will eventually meet up with opportunity. You'll never know exactly who your ideal mate will be or when you'll find them. However, it's unlikely you'll find them if you're not an active participant in life. You must be celebrating life by actually enjoying it. When you're enjoying the experiences of life, you're living in a state of love, trusting your intuition, and are willing to take risks.

Nothing except paying taxes, breathing, and death has any kind of guarantee. If you're not open to taking a few risks, reaching out to other people, or recognizing opportunity when it shows up, then it's difficult for others to enter your space because you're living in a state of fear. You'll attract people who mirror how you actually feel, not what you want or think you feel.

I realize it's not an easy journey. But if you view it as a mystery, believing you'll find the missing piece while enjoying the search, you'll find rewards throughout your journey. As Tennyson wrote: " 'Tis better to have loved and lost, than never to have loved at all."

To educate the heart, one must be willing to go out of himself and to come into loving contact with others.

JAMES FREEMAN CLARKE

Resources

I've spent years counseling and helping people create the lives they've wanted. I've taken the initiative to research the best ways for people to heal spiritually and emotionally so they can learn to listen to, trust, and follow their own intuition. By doing this you can attract anything you want, including your ideal mate.

Listed below are additional books you may want to read to enhance your growth.

Anatomy of the Spirit by Caroline Myss
Are You the One for Me? by Barbara DeAngelis
The Bridge Across Forever by Richard Bach
Creative Visualization by Shakti Gawain
Create Your Own Future by Linda Georgian
Feel the Fear and Do It Anyway by Susan Jeffers
Finding Love by Paula Peisner Coxe
Finding True Love by Daphne Rose Kingman
Mars and Venus on a Date by John Gray
Negotiating Love by Riki Robbins Jones
The Path to Love by Deepak Chopra

Real Moments for Lovers by Barbara DeAngelis
The Real Rules by Barbara DeAngelis
The Seven Spiritual Laws of Success by Deepak Chopra
Taming Your Gremlin by Richard D. Carson
Your Guardian Angels by Linda Georgian

Index